Robert Irwin's Power Tips for Buying a House for Less

Other McGraw-Hill Books by Robert Irwin

Tips and Traps When Buying a Condo, Co-op, or Townhouse

Tips and Traps When Mortgage Hunting

Buying a Home on the Internet

Pocket Guide for Home Buyers

Tips and Traps When Buying a Home

Tips and Traps When Selling a Home

Tips and Traps for Making Money in Real Estate

*Buy, Rent, & Hold: How to Make Money in a "Cold"
Real Estate Market*

How to Find Hidden Real Estate Bargains

The McGraw-Hill Real Estate Handbook

Tips and Traps When Negotiating Real Estate

Tips and Traps When Renovating Your Home

Robert Irwin's Power Tips for Buying a House for Less

Robert Irwin

McGraw-Hill

New York   San Francisco   Washington, D.C.   Auckland   Bogotá
Caracas   Lisbon   London   Madrid   Mexico City   Milan
Montreal   New Delhi   San Juan   Singapore
Sydney   Tokyo   Toronto

For Rita,
without whom all the buying and selling
would have been meaningless.

McGraw-Hill

A Division of The McGraw·Hill Companies

Copyright © 2000 by The McGraw-Hill Companies, Inc. All rights reserved. Printed in the United States of America. Except as permitted under the United States Copyright Act of 1976, no part of this publication may be reproduced or distributed in any form or by any means, or stored in a data base or retrieval system, without the prior written permission of the publisher.

2 3 4 5 6 7 8 9 0   AGM/AGM   0 9 8 7 6 5 4 3 2 1 0

ISBN 0-07-135687-8

It was set in Baskerville per the BSF TTS design by Pat Caruso and Joanne Morbit of the Professional Book Group's composition unit, Hightstown, N.J.

Printed and bound by Quebecor World/Martinsburg.

McGraw-Hill books are available at special quantity discounts to use as premiums and sales promotions, or for use in corporate training programs. For more information, please write to the Director of Special Sales, Professional Publishing, McGraw-Hill, Two Penn Plaza, New York, NY 10121-2298. Or contact your local bookstore.

This book contains the author's opinions. Some material in this book may be affected by changes in the law (or changes in interpretations of the law) or changes in the market conditions since the manuscript was prepared. Therefore, the accuracy and completness of the information contained in this book and the opinions based on it cannot be guaranteed. Neither the author nor the publisher is engaged in rendering investment, legal, tax, accounting, or other similar professional services. If these services are required, the reader should obtain them from a competent professional.

Contents

Introduction   vii

1. Plan Before You Purchase   1

1. Avoid Neighborhoods With Lots of Rentals   2
2. Get "In Bed" With a Legitimate Lender   4
3. Avoid Inappropriate Neighborhoods   7
4. Stay Away From "Low Percentile" Schools   9
5. Check the Graffiti Index   11
6. Never Go Far for a Bottle of Milk   13
7. Use a Buyer's Agent   15
8. Look for a Strong Home Owners Association   21
9. Get a Real Estate Map   23
10. Build a Plan of Action   26

2. Strategies for a Hot Market   31

11. Do Your Own Canvassing in a Hot Market   32
12. Find the One Agent Who Can Deliver   34
13. Track Down Elusive Sellers   37
14. Offer More Than the Asking Price   40
15. Avoid Multiple Offers   43
16. Get Your Offer in Early Before Others Arrive   46
17. Buy Sight Unseen   47
18. Look for "As Is" Homes   50
19. Look for Fixer-Uppers   54
20. Look for "Out of Favor" Homes   57
21. Check for the FSBO Effect   60
22. Take a Backup Position   64
23. Make a Cash-Only Offer   68

3. Tactics for Successful Offers   73

24. Never Give Sellers More Than 24 Hours to Sign   74
25. Work the Contingencies   77
26. Start With a Small Deposit   83
27. Always Demand Inspections and Disclosures   88
28. Never Stop Negotiating   92
29. Find Sellers Who Are Highly Motivated   97
30. Sweeten a Low Offer With Better Terms   101

4. Profiting in a Normal or Cold Market   105

31. Look for More Expensive Homes Than You Qualify For   106
32. Low-Ball Your First Offer   110
33. Look for REOs and Foreclosures   113
34. Look for Auctions   118
35. Work With Upside-Down Sellers   121

5. Get Lenders to Work for You   125

36. Get the Right Type of Mortgage   126
37. Don't Pay a Fee to a Mortgage Broker   137
38. Lock In the Loan   141
39. Don't Agree to a Prepayment Penalty   144
40. Lower Your Interest Rate by Getting a Shorter Term   147
41. Don't Take Out 125 Percent Loans   151
42. Don't Pay "Garbage" Costs   155
43. Trade Points for Interest and Vice Versa   158
44. Use Creative Financing to Your Advantage   161
45. Get An Asset-Based Loan   165
46. Get a Mortgage on Another Property   168
47. If You're Self-Employed, Get a Low-Doc, No-Doc Loan   171

6. Easier Closings   175

48. Have Sellers Pay Your Costs   176
49. Finance Your Closing Costs   179
50. Avoid Hidden Buyers Fees   182

7. When Buying a Brand New Home   189

51. Be First in Line   190
52. Buy Homes in Stock   198
53. Get Upgrades, but Don't Buy Them Separately   200

Checklists   203
Glossary   211
Index   223

Introduction

Buying a home is not like buying anything else. For example, when you purchase a jar of mayonnaise in the store, the price is fixed, no arguing. When you buy a home, negotiating (arguing) over the price is simply understood as part of making the purchase.

When you buy a car, you know that the value is going to drop significantly the moment you drive it off the lot. When you buy a home, the anticipation (or at least the hope) is that it will go up in value from the moment of purchase.

When you purchase a stock, the process is swift and perfectly defined, and usually has no hitches. On the other hand, when you are purchasing a home, the process itself can take a month or more, has all sort of hoops you have to jump through, and is fraught with perils.

As I said, buying a home is not like buying anything else. It is an unique experience.

Unfortunately, that experience can be a bad one if you make a mistake. You can pay too much and as a result be unable to resell for a profit (or have to take a loss). You can get bad financing that will cost you extra money out of your pocket every month. You can get onerous sales conditions (such as a short balloon payment or excessive closing fees) that you keep worrying about even after you move into the property. You could even buy a home with a serious hidden defect that makes it almost impossible to resell. In short, the things that can go wrong for the unwary buyer in a home purchase are myriad.

Further, the problems can be exacerbated by changing market conditions. When the housing market is red hot, there are often multiple offers on the same property, sometimes on the very day it is listed. You can spend hours and weeks looking for the right home that always seems to be sold when you finally find it. And prices keep moving upward—always, it seems, just out of reach.

On the other hand, the market can and has declined. Suddenly there can be a large inventory of homes for sale with prices remaining static or even falling down. When the market is cold, no matter how much you offer, you're afraid it will be too much because tomorrow the house will be worth less.

All of which is to say that buying a home is sufficiently important that you need to do it right, get the best deal, pay the least amount of money, and avoid the pitfalls. After your purchase, you want to sleep comfortably at night knowing that you weren't "taken for a ride," that you got at minimum a good house for a fair price and, hopefully, that you actually got a "steal"! It all comes down to simply knowing what you should do.

There are lots of books out there that explain the home buying process. But, if you're a savvy buyer, you want to know more than the rules of the game. You want to know how to win at it.

That's the business of this book.

What Should You Do?

In the following chapters we'll go into the positive, assertive things you should do to get the best deal when you buy your home. The chapters are arranged in the natural order of making a purchase. For example, the first chapter deals with getting yourself ready and finding the home. It explains the true value and use of "preapproval," of looking in areas where you will enjoy living and which amplify your chances of being able to resell for a profit. (Yes, "Location, location, loacation" are the watchwords of real estate—but they won't do you much good unless you know exactly how to apply them.) The chapter also goes into details on how to find an agent and how to plan your attack when searching for a house.

When the Market's Strong

Since the turn of the century, the real estate market has been strong, bouncing back after the recession of the early to mid-1990s. If you're buying into this market, you need to know how to get a house before it's sold out from under you. Chapter 2 tells you how to proceed.

The second chapter also explains how to deal with evasive sellers (who would rather not get a single quick offer in the hopes of waiting to get multiple offers), how to win at an auction, why you should sometimes offer more than the purchase price, and in general where to find the best home for the dollar when all the houses seem priced too high.

Getting an Offer Accepted

Regardless of market conditions, there are tactics that you will want to use to "pressure" the seller to go along with your offer. Chapter 3 explains why you must limit the seller's time for acceptance, start with a small deposit, trade terms for price, and look for those elusive "highly motivated" sellers. It also shows you how to work the contingencies in the contract to leave you an all-important escape hatch.

When the Market's Weak

Despite the strength of the current real estate market, booms don't last forever. While what goes up doesn't necessarily come all the way back down, many times it does decline a bit. By the time you read this book, we could be into the next cycle with the real estate market declining. What do you do when you need a home and prices are stagnant or falling?

Chapter 4 details the art of "lowballing" an offer in order to get the price down, of working with sellers who owe more than their house is worth, and of finding and winning at auctions. It also brings to light the sometimes hidden world of foreclosures and REOs (property that lenders own and want to sell in the worst way).

Getting a Better Loan

The common assumption is that the lenders have all the power and hence can control everything that happens in the marketplace. Not so.

While it's true that you normally have to go to an institutional lender (such as a bank or mortgage banker) to get a home loan, the market is extremely competitive. Mortgage lenders are constantly revamping their mortgage offerings, attempting to make them even more appealing to consumers.

Chapter 5 shows you how to push your lender to get a better mortgage. It explains about garbage fees and how to challenge them. It shows how to avoid paying a prepayment penalty and how to get a lower interest rate. It even explains when you should trade out points for a higher interest rate!

Close It Quickly

Of course, eventually every real estate transaction must be closed. And there are right and wrong ways to accomplish this. Chapter 6 explains what you should do to avoid extra closing fees. It goes on to show you how to get your lender to finance your closing costs. And it even suggests a way to get the seller to pay for those closing costs!

Or Buy New

Finally, your choice may not be to buy a resale, but to move into the new home market. Here, you want to get the upgrades, but not pay an arm or a leg for them. And if there are 500 applicants and 50 homes, you want to be sure that you're one of the successful buyers. Chapter 7 details what you must do to be a successful new home buyer.

53 in All

In all this book offers you 53 power tips for buying your next home. What's magical about the number "53?" Nothing at all, it just happens to be the number of useful tips that I've discovered every buyer should know.

1
Plan Before You Purchase

Power Tip 1
Avoid Neighborhoods With
Lots of Rentals

Chances are there always will be some rental homes in any neighborhood you are considering. There's nothing wrong with this at all. However, when the ratio of tenants to owners gets too high, it can have a serious affect on the property values of surrounding homes.

The reason has to do with "pride of ownership." Tenants are usually short-timers living in someone else's home. As a result, they are less motivated to maintain a yard or fix things up as they deteriorate. They figure it's the owner-landlord's responsibility.

On the other hand owner-landlords will sometimes defer maintenance or do less expensive work figuring that it's "only a rental, not my own home!"As a result, rental properties may stand out as noticeable different from surrounding homes, and not in a good way. This is not to say that there are no good tenants or landlords. Most keep properties in great shape. It's just that some don't. An occasional rental home in a neighborhood will barely be noticed. However, if every third or fourth home is a rental, you will see the difference.

If there are a lot of rentals in a neighborhood, you have to ask yourself, "Why are there so many tenant-occupied homes? There can be many answers. Sometimes it's because it's a transient neighborhood... people stay only a short time on their way to a job change or a better neighborhood. Other times it's because former owners wanted to sell, but couldn't. So they took the alternative of moving away and renting out their old property. Either way, you have to ask yourself, "is this a neighborhood I want to buy into?"

As a general rule, areas with high tenant ratios tend to look shoddier, have more complaints about noise and traffic, and are more difficult to resell.

Too many tenants in a condo development spells trouble. Often lenders will refuse to offer condo mortgages when the tenant ratio is 25 percent or higher.

Ask Your Agent About Rentals
in the Area

Often agents know which neighborhoods have an overpopulation of rental properties. If you ask, they'll tell you. Also, if there's a home-owner's association, it can often tell you how many homes are rentals and how many are owner-occupied.

Walk the neighborhood. If you see well-kept homes interspersed with shoddy properties, ask yourself if these are rentals. You may even want to knock on a few doors to confirm your suspicions. If you say you're thinking of buying in the area and are just curious, most people will willing give you this information.

> Short-term tenants tend to put a heavier strain on amenities such as a community golf course, tennis courts, or a swimming pool.

Don't Worry as Much About Rental
Ratios in Vacation Homes

An exception is vacation or recreational property. Here, the major-ity of properties may be second homes. They may be used only a few months or even a few weeks out of the year. As a result, the owners rent them out, often on a short-term basis. Sometimes as many as half the properties are rented out weekly. But the area is set up to handle short-term occupants.

> Co-ops are an exception to many rental concerns, since the ownership structure allows the board of directors more control over subletting units than is found in other types of housing.

Power Tip 2
Get "In Bed" With a
Legitimate Lender

The old way of beginning a house hunt was to check out homes for sale; begin looking at property. That's a mistake. The first step today has nothing to do with the home itself. Rather, it involves locating a legitimate lender and getting "preapproved."

Preapproval means that you actually apply for a mortgage, even though you haven't yet found a home to buy. You go through the steps of filling out an application, getting a credit report, and (if you're thorough) getting verifications of your employment and available cash on deposit. Armed with this information, you can get preapproval from a lender upx to a maximum loan amount.

> There are two kinds of preapproval: conditional and uncondi-tional. *Conditional* means that the lender will give you a mort-gage provided you fulfill certain demands such as meeting income, cash available, or credit requirements. *Unconditional* means you've already met these requirements, and you'll get the mortgage no matter what. Unconditional preapprovals carry far more weight with sellers, for obvious reasons.

There are two very good reasons for getting preapproved. First, it lets you know how much house you can afford. The preapproval let-ter usually states the maximum loan you can qualify for. (Since loan size is a function of interest rates, some lenders will instead state the maximum monthly payment you qualify for.) From here it's just a simple step to determine your maximum price. (Maximum loan plus down payment equals maximum price.)

Unless you're planning to pay cash for your home, this is vital information. Armed with a preapproval letter, you will know exactly the price range you should be in. The information helps you (and your real estate agent) select properties you can afford.

You can avoid the preapproval process if you pay cash. A little more than 12 percent of all home buyers pay cash, the majority of them for higher-priced homes. But you will find that a letter from your bank showing your funds on deposit is helpful in convincing a seller you're for real.

Second, when you do find a home, you can present a preapproval letter from your legitimate lender to the sellers. This lets them know up front that you will qualify for a loan to buy their property. Preapproval can be essential when you're in a highly competitive market.

Use a "Legitimate" Lender

I say "legitimate" because anyone can qualify you for a mortgage. Your real estate agent can, I can, your brother-in-law can. We can all issue you a letter saying that you are qualified to obtain a mortgage for X dollars. But what does such a letter of qualification mean?

It means nothing, because there's nothing standing behind it. Chances are your agent or your brother-in-law isn't going to lend you any money. So their saying you're qualified to get a loan carries little weight.

If you get a letter stating you are preapproved for a mortgage from an actual lender (such as a bank or mortgage banker), it's a different story. The letter is similar to a letter of credit. It means the lender has already agreed to give you a mortgage. All you need to do is find a house to put it on.

Legitimate lenders (all of which should be listed in your phone book under mortgages) include:

Banks

Mortgage bankers

Credit unions

Savings and loan associations (if you can find them)

Mortgage brokers (when issued through a lender)

On-line lenders (mortgage sites on the Internet)

Mortgage brokers are the most popular source of mortgages today. Be aware, however, that their fee is paid by the lender, not you. Your only up-front cost for dealing with a mortgage broker should be the fee for your credit report. Run away from a mortgage broker who wants a fee from you (usually expressed as one point or more going to the broker). Check out Chapter 5, on lending, for more information.

It's important to understand that a letter from a mortgage broker alone does not carry the weight of a letter from a bank or mortgage banker. If you deal with a mortgage broker (and most people do, these days), you'll want to be sure the broker secures your preapproval directly from a lender, such as a bank.

Be Prepared to Offer Your Financial Vitals

The preapproval application usually consists of 60 or so questions that delve into all your finances. You may feel as though you don't want to disclose some things. But if you want a mortgage, you'll just have to allow the lender to get to know you, financially speaking.

Be prepared to come up with documentation as well. (There are some low-doc, no-doc loans available—check into Chapter 5.) At a minimum, you'll need a recent paystub, your bank account statement, your rental lease or current mortgage payment stub, and a list of your credit accounts (credit cards, loans, and so on). Once you supply the needed information and undergo a credit check, it's only a short time until the preapproval letter is ready.

I recently was talking with a real estate agent who said that preapproval letters meant nothing, since these days virtually every buyer had one. On the contrary, I told her, if most buyers have one, then it means the letters are vital, for the buyer who doesn't have one will have little chance of convincing sellers to take his or her offer.

Power Tip 3
Avoid Inappropriate
Neighborhoods

Although your primary purpose in purchasing a home usually is to provide shelter for you and your family, it is a mistake to overlook the investment factor. Indeed, the home may very well be one of the biggest investments you'll ever make. Therefore, it is vital to buy a home that you will be able to resell easily and at a profit. And that has most to do with neighborhood. (Remember: "Location, location, location!")

A good neighborhood will have obvious qualities. The houses will be neat and well kept with manicured lawns and shrubs. The streets will be wide without too much traffic. There will be parks and playgrounds nearby. It will be appealing and you'll want to live there. Hopefully, so too will the next buyer when it comes time to resell.

An inappropriate neighborhood (for price appreciation) can be more difficult to identify. You may have to do some homework to come up with reasons not to buy in an area. There are at least five reasons that I would consider:

Neighborhood Problems to Avoid

1. Poor schools
2. High crime
3. Little to no shopping
4. Poor access to transportation
5. High number of rental

We'll discuss these in the next group of tips. However, there's one additional factor that could disqualify a neighborhood for you and it has nothing to do with price appreciation. The area may simply not be appropriate for your lifestyle.

For example, if you have young children, you may not want to move into an established neighborhood where all the kids either are older or have grown up and left home. There won't be playmates around for your children.

Similarly, if you're an empty nester, you probably won't want to buy in a neighborhood of brand-new homes where there are mostly families with little kids. You may not want the noise and activity that the youngsters provide.

On the other hand, you may not want a house at all. Rather, your desire may be for the shared lifestyle offered by a condo, townhouse, or co-op. Here, in addition to a usually lower initial price (and reduced sales price when you resell), you often get extra amenities. These may include a recreation center, swimming pool and spa, tennis courts, or even a golf course.

> If you're looking at a condo, townhouse, or co-op, keep in mind that historically these have been the first to drop in value during a recession and the last to recoup value during a boom period. Of course, there are exceptions. Also be aware that living in one of these developments offers a different and more controlled lifestyle than you're likely to experience owning a single-family home. So be sure it's what you want before you leap in.

If the shared-lifestyle form of home ownership appeals to you, check out my new book, *Tips and Traps When Buying Condos, Townhomes, and Co-ops* (McGraw-Hill, 2000).

Power Tip 4
Stay Away From "Low Percentile" Schools

Lets face it: Not all public schools are created equal. Some are great, and some are terrible. And there are a host in between. The question is: Should you care when you're looking to buy a new home?

You certainly should. Experience has shown that nothing influences home appreciation as much as the quality of neighborhood schools. Invariably homes in neighborhoods with good schools go up most rapidly in price. On the other side of the coin, those in neighborhoods with poor schools languish or actually decline in price. If you want to come close to guaranteeing that the home you buy will have the highest appreciation, buy in an area with top schools.

There's a logical reason. Families with children are very concerned about education. They try to live where the schools are good, creating a strong demand for homes in surrounding neighborhoods. And home prices go up because of that demand.

But how do you determine how good the schools really are? After all, there isn't a national rating system for schools. Or is there?

In effect, there is. These days students in elementary, intermediate, and high schools in virtually every state take standardized tests. The overall scores are given as local, state, and sometimes national percentiles, and they are public information. You can get them by school district, by individual school, and even by grade. Some states, such as California, even rank their school!

Understand What the Scores Really Say

It's important to understand that scores in any given year, school, or grade can be high or low. It is a mistake to look at individual scores. What you want to look at is how a school and a school district measure up over time. You want to see trends. For example, some schools and districts consistently score in the 80th percentile year after year. Others score in the 20th percentile. If you have kids, which schools would you want them to attend? Most people feel, like you, that they want their kids to go to the better (higher percentile) schools. And property values in the surrounding neighborhoods benefit.

But how high is good enough? The top districts and schools in the country regularly score in the 85th percentile and higher both within the state and by national norms (when available). However, be aware that these schools are often in elite neighborhoods where home prices are anywhere from two to five times the median price for the rest of the country. (Currently the median price for a home nationwide is about $150,000 and is climbing rapidly.)

> Districts and schools that score above the 60th percentile should be considered good, with a positive influence on their surrounding neighborhoods. Scores between 50 and 60 are probably neutral. Scores below the 50th percentile could have an adverse effect on housing values.

Check Out the Scores

You can get the standardized test scores by checking in at the administrative office of any school district. Or, more conveniently, you can get them on the Internet. Use a search engine such as Yahoo.com or Excite.com. To find Web sites for local, county, and state school districts. Also, search under the school name.

Power Tip 5
Check the Graffiti Index

Crime used to be the number-one domestic concern for most people in America. However, as crime in all categories diminished into the early 21st century, it has become less of an issue. Nevertheless, most people desire to live in a relatively crime-free environment. And they will generally pay more to be able to do so.

> I have gone out with real estate people who, when I ask about crime rates, say, "All neighborhoods have crime. You can't avoid it." Maybe not, but you can at least lower your odds of been affected. At the same time, you can improve your odds of price appreciation in the home you buy.

This is the reason so many gated communities are sprouting up all across the country. Homes in gated communities are generally worth between 5 and 10 percent more (assuming the same-size lot and house and other factors being equal) than homes just outside the gates. The presumption is that the crooks can't get into the gated communities. (Interestingly, in some areas the crime rates inside gated communities are not significantly lower than those outside!)

It's also the reason that communities with low crime rates often advertise the fact. They know that more people will be attracted to their area.

All of which is to say that areas with high crime rates tend to have slower appreciation and lower housing values than those with low crime rates. If you didn't already want to live in a low crime rate community, here's a big reason to do so.

Check Out the Crime Rates

The number of crimes committed by category (burglary, rape, murder, and so on) is readily available from almost all police departments. Indeed, most bigger departments have it computerized and listed by location, even broken down to specific blocks. If, for example, you're interested in buying a home at 2234 Maple Street, you can call the police department and usually get a printed list of all crimes reported in the 2200 block of Maple Street within the last six months as well as crimes in the surrounding neighborhood.

> To get crime statistics, ask for the public affairs officer of your local police department. Some of the larger police departments have their own Web sites and publish these statistics on the Internet.

Look for Graffiti

I have my own method of checking out crime in neighborhoods. I call it my "Graffiti Index." I drive around the neighborhood looking for graffiti on fences and walls. The more graffiti I find, the more crime I assume there to be in the neighborhood.

Is there really a correlation between the amount of graffiti and crime in the area? I believe there is. Of course, lack of graffiti on walls doesn't mean that there is no crime in the area. Some crimes are random; others (including murder) are deliberate acts, often crimes of passion, and leave no neighborhood untouched.

But community crimes such as burglary, theft, assault, and rape are greater in areas where there is heavy graffiti. If you don't believe it, check it out with your local police department.

Of course, these days it can be argued that all neighborhoods have some graffiti. It's almost inevitable. Yes, but in good communities, the neighbors are out in force the minute graffiti appears to remove or paint over it. It's not allowed to remain there. The communities to beware of are those where neighbors are hesitant to come out and remove graffiti for fear of gang or other reprisals.

When I drive through a neighborhood and see no graffiti at all, I feel safe and confident that crime probably won't be a negative issue in price appreciation. If I drive through and see lots of graffiti, it raises a red flag for me.

If there's just a little graffiti, I will come back a few nights later to see if it's been taken care of by the neighbors. If it has, I assume that it's a strong neighborhood and feel good about it. If it remains there week after week, however, I begin to get really concerned about how badly home values may be affected.

Power Tip 6
Never Go Far for a
Bottle of Milk

None of us is self-sufficient this days. We don't raise our own food, make our own clothes, or even entertain each other (movies and television do that). So no matter where you buy your home, you'll need to be able to get out to purchase things. The closer to shopping you are, the better.

> Close doesn't mean next door. When a home is right next to a mall or shopping center, the activity, lights, and noise are a detraction. It's better that shopping be at least half a dozen blocks away than right next door.

The same applies to your work and to other places to which you travel. You want to be able to get out and onto the roadways or mass transit as quickly and easily as possible. All of which is to say you would be well advised to buy a home that has easy access to transportation and is close to a wide variety of shopping. Unfortunately, with builders putting up tracts farther and farther away from cities, that's increasingly difficult to do.

If you buy far away from transportation and shopping, you run the risk of having property that is difficult to resell. Potential buyers will evaluate how close-in your home is. Generally speaking, the closer to work and shopping a property is, the greater its value.

Be Sure It's Really Accessible When You Need It

Accessibility is a funny thing. Sometimes it's not there even when you think it is. For example, in Southern California you may be within half a mile of a freeway entrance. That would normally be considered good access. However, if that freeway happens to be Interstate 405 or 5, it could mean that you will zip on only to find cars moving at a snail's pace. (Some estimates are that by the year 2002 the average speed on freeways in Southern California will be 10 mph!)

Many people judge accessibility these days in terms of time, not distance. For example, shopping is only 20 minutes away. Or it's only 40 minutes to a major industrial area (read, lots of jobs). On the other hand, in some areas of the country people travel an hour or two each way or even longer to get to and from work. The reason, of course, is that the further away, the less expensive the housing.

Another way of putting it is that the closer in, the more valuable the housing—both when you buy and when you resell.

Power Tip 7
Use a Buyer's Agent

Traditionally real estate buyers looked at homes with an agent, without much regard for whom that agent actually represented. Often buyers would stop at a house for sale and be shown the property by an agent sitting there. If they liked it, that agent would then write up their offer.

Problems abound with this method. Who does that agent truly represent? Is it you, the buyer? Or is it the seller? In most cases it's the seller.

When an agent lists a home, he or she normally becomes the agent of the seller. That means that this agent's purpose is not only to find a buyer, but to get as high a price and as good terms as possible *for the seller.* Of course, as a buyer, that's exactly the opposite of what you want. You want the lowest price and the best terms for you.

Okay, you may be thinking to yourself. The agents I've gone out with aren't the ones who actually listed the home. Aren't they on my side?

Not necessarily. As subagents of the lister, they may owe their bond of loyalty, their fiduciary relationship, to the seller as well. In other words, every agent you deal with could be an agent of the seller! You might have no one in your corner.

Ask the Agent Whom He or She Represents

The way to find an agent who represents you and not the seller is to ask whom the agent represents. The agent may declare either for the seller or for you, or in some strange cases for both. (More to say about this in a moment.)

It important to understand that payment of the agent's fee does not determine who the agent represents. While the seller may pay the commission, the agent can still declare you, the buyer, as his or her fiduciary.

In many states today, before you make an offer, the agent must present you with a written declaration stating whom he or she represents. Take this statement to heart. If the agent represents the seller, be careful. Anything you say can and will be used against you!

For example, if you offer $150,000 for a property, yet tell a seller's agent that you're really willing to pay $160,000, that agent is duty bound to tell the seller that you're willing to pay more. When that happens, just how seriously do you think the seller will treat your $150,000 offer?

On the other hand, if you are working with a buyer's agent, that agent is required *not* to tell the seller of your top price. Further, if your buyer's agent discovers that the seller is willing to take $10,000 less than the asking price, the agent is duty bound to tell you of that fact!

It's easy to see why it's beneficial to work with a buyer's agent.

Be Careful of the "Dual" Agent

Some agents will declare that they represent both buyers and sellers. This is often the case when the same agent both lists the property and submits your offer. There is nothing legally wrong here. Indeed, in the strange ethics of business, there is nothing ethically wrong with it as well. However, for my money it's simply a theoretical fabrication that makes no sense.

No one can serve two masters, and no agent can represent buyers and sellers as well as an agent who declares for just one party or the other. That's why if you're working with a dual agent (one representing both buyers and sellers), be on your guard. Don't count on the agent always being in your corner.

> You may want to work with a dual agent in order to get a savings in commission. An agent who represents both buyer and seller, doesn't have to split the commission with other agents and may be willing to throw in some of that commission, which, in effect, will get you a reduced price.

You'll See More Properties With a Buyer's Agent

There's a second reason for using a buyer's agent. You probably will be shown more diverse properties. A buyer's agent doesn't necessarily rely on the seller to be paid. Instead, he or she counts on you for that. (More to say about this shortly.) Hence, that agent is willing to show you all sorts of properties, including those that are "for sale by owner" and others that the sellers are thinking about listing, but haven't yet signed on with a listing agreement. The buyer's agent may also show you bank-owned properties (repossessions) for which the bank is not offering a broker's commission.

A seller's agent generally will want to show you only listed properties, ones on which he or she can collect a commission. (Agents are supposed to show you all properties, but in the real world, why show you a property on which they can't get paid?) Of course, it all depends on how good the buyer's agent is and what contacts he or she has. Some buyer's agents are nothing more than seller's agents wearing a different hat. Others really do go out of their way for the buyers.

Don't Pay a Buyer's Agent an Up-Front Fee

A true buyer's agent will want you to sign an agreement in which you agree to pay a commission for finding you a property. It's sort of like a listing agreement, only instead of listing property, it's listing you!

Many buyers are outraged by this concept, having lived for decades under a system where the sellers always paid the commission. Nevertheless, it's something at least worth considering, particularly if the buyer's agent can get you the house you want at a significant savings.

> In most cases the commission is paid by the seller even if you use a buyer's agent. Usually what happens is that the buyer's agent works out a "cobroking" deal with the seller's agent for half of the listing commission—and the commission to you is zero. That's the way it works in most cases, but not always.

It's very important that you carefully read any agreement a buyer's agent wants you to sign. You should particularly be on the watch for the following.

1. *Any demand that you pay the buyer's agent an up-front fee.* Some agreements state that you will pay the buyer's agent $1,000 (more or less) to commence finding a property for you. If you eventually buy, the advance is taken from the commission. If you don't, you lose the money.

The obvious problem here is that the agreement ties you to the agent. If you don't like the way the agent is proceeding, you will be reluctant to drop out and go elsewhere because you've got money invested. Further, why should you pay anything at all if the agent can't find you a property you want to buy?

A buyer's agent should work just like a seller's agent. No money up front.

2. *Any demand that you pay a commission to a buyer's agent when you purchase a listed property.* If the property is listed, the buyer's agent should work out a split in commission with the listing agent. If you agree to pay a commission regardless, then there's no incentive for the buyer's agent to work out a split. It's so much easier to just come to you for the money.

A second concern here is that the buyer's agent could, potentially, get two commissions: one from you and another from the seller.

3. *Any demand that you pay a commission even if you don't buy a property.* With a seller's agent, the rule is that the commission is owed when a buyer is found who is "ready, willing, and able to purchase," even if the seller then refuses to go through with a deal. With a buyer's agent, something similar can be demanded—you owe a commission when a home is found that matches the price and terms you want. Only with selecting homes it's not as simple as price and terms. You may not like the place regardless of how good a deal it is financially. You shouldn't have to pay a commission unless you go through with the purchase. (An exception is if you hire an agent to find a specific model home in a specific tract, setting out all details down to exposure and color as well as price and terms.)

4. *Any demand that you work exclusively with the buyer's agent for an indefinite or a long period of time.* Just as with a listing agent, it's not unreasonable for a buyer's agent to want you to work exclusively with him or her in finding a house. After all, why should the agent spend a lot of time looking for you, if you then simply hop over and purchase through a different agent? If you want to work with a buyer's agent, you should give the agent your loyalty, whether it's in a contract or not.

On the other hand, your loyalty should have a time limit. If the agent can't find the house of your dreams for you within, say, 30 or 60 days, you should have the right to look with someone else.

A good time limit when listing a home with an agent is 90 days. However, with a buyer's agent, I feel that 30 days is a good starting time limit. Working hard, you should be able to get a good idea of the market by that time. And if you decide you want to continue working with the agent, you can always renew.

Without a formal agreement, you can simply drop the buyer's agent and work with someone else. With a formal agreement, it's not so simple. While the agreement is in force, you could owe the buyer's agent a commission even if you buy through another agent, or even if you buy directly from the seller with no agent involved! As I said, be sure you carefully read any agreement before you sign. Make sure you understand and want the terms it locks you into.

Should You Pay an Agent's Commission When You're a Buyer?

That, of course, is the dilemma. No buyer wants to pay a commission. Yet it could be worthwhile if the agent is terrific, can show you just the property you want, and can negotiate a terrific deal for you.

Don't be constrained by old-time thinking. Do what's required to get the best deal for yourself.

Be sure that you feel comfortable with any agent you're with. You want that agent to have just the right combination of assertiveness (to get a good deal for you from the buyers) and compliance (to go along with your wishes). On the one hand, you don't want the agent pushing you into a home you really don't want, just to get the commission. On the other, you don't want the agent fawning over your every wish to the point of leading you into absurd offers that sellers will never accept. The agent should be part teacher (showing you the market), part financial adviser (helping you understand how you'll pay for it all), and part confidant (listening to your heartfelt housing desires, as well as tipping you off to any advantages you may have over the sellers). If you find you really don't like your agent, it's time to look for another.

Power Tip 8
Look for a Strong Home
Owners Association

Home owners associations (HOA), as anyone who has lived under the jurisdiction of one knows, are a pain in the you know where. However, they are also what maintains and accelerates price appreciation in a neighborhood. So you should try to buy within a strong one, if you can stand it!

Home owners associations automatically go with any condo or townhouse development. Co-ops have a governing board of the corporation, which wields even more authority. However, some single-family homes also belong to a neighborhood HOA.

You normally can't join an HOA. Rather, provision for it must be in the deed to your property, in the CC&Rs (conditions, covenants, and restrictions). These run with the title to the property and are usually placed there when the home is built. They may, however, be placed later when an entire neighborhood comes together to form an association.

The purpose of the HOA is to maintain the common facilities (if any) such as paths, parking areas, and swimming pool. In addition, a very important function is to maintain architectural control over the neighborhood—to keep things looking good. Thus, usually the most important force in any HOA is the architectural committee.

Even if you have a single-family house, if you're in an HOA, you probably need its permission to change the color of paint on your house, put on any addition, change the shape of a window, or even relocate shrubbery in your front yard! Generally speaking, you can't do anything to the exterior of your property without the specific permission of the HOA.

In many HOAs, the architectural committee comes by twice a year to check the appearance of your home. If your lawn looks bad, your paint is worn out, or your roof has shingles missing, you may be told to fix it up or risk a fine and, for repeated offenses, a lien or lawsuit!

For doing all this, the HOA demands a monthly (sometimes annual) assessment. In single-family organizations where there is no community property, only architectural control, the fee may be only a small amount, perhaps $20 or $30 a month. In condos where there is lots of community property, it could be much higher, say $200 to $300 a month.

> The monthly HOA assessment will be a factor when it comes time to resell. Homes in associations with high monthly assessments are harder to sell than those in associations with low ones.

The assessment may be particularly high if there was bad management in the past, if insufficient reserves were set aside for replacement of items as they wear out, or if lawsuits have been filed by owners or others. Occasionally, there will be short-term high assessments to cover these items, after which the monthly or annual assessment drops down to more normal levels.

If you're new to this game, you may be wondering why anyone would want to live under the draconian rule and the extra costs of an HOA. After all, aren't all Americans supposed to be free spirits, desiring, even demanding, that everyone do as he or she pleases?

Indeed. On the other hand, there's the profit motive. Neighborhoods with strong HOAs generally keep their prices better and show stronger appreciation than surrounding areas without HOAs. One reason is that they look so good. Another reason is that with a strong HOA you don't have to fear that an unruly neighbor will paint her house purple or will let his yard go to seed. The HOA is there to protect you.

> There are some limitations here. Except in the case of a co-op, the HOA may be able to do very little if a neighbor plants a tall tree blocking your view, throws loud parties, or has barking dogs. Calling the police, in the case of the latter two, may be your only option.

Given a choice between buying a home with a strong HOA and one with none at all, I'd buy the property with the HOA every time. I like the protections and the maintenance of property values it affords. On the other hand, you may value your freedom more.

Power Tip 9
Get a Real Estate Map

What's a real estate map?

It looks like a regular map of the area where you want to purchase your next home. Only marked on it are all the houses you've seen (along with their price) as well as those neighborhoods that you think are potentially the best for you.

It's a fact that after you've seen a couple of homes and gone out with an agent a few times, locations and properties will tend to fog together. Was it the house on Maple Street that had the big garage, or the one on Walnut? How much was the asking price for the home on Westpoint Drive? Was that the one we thought they were asking too much for? Or did it seem like the good deal?

Often, in the haste to see as many homes as possible as quickly as you can, you'll actually pass right over the right home for you. Later on, something in the back of you mind will nag you about that place, if only you could remember how much it cost and where it was located.

It's a fact that your impressions will be tainted by the properties you've previously seen. For example, if you walk through an elegantly presented home with a marble entry, granite-countertopped kitchen, and vaulted ceilings—you get the idea—you're going to be mightily impressed. Of course, you may not possibly be able afford this home. Next you walk through a modest home you can afford that doesn't have marble, granite, or vaulted ceilings. By comparison, the second home will seem shabby and you might not seriously consider it, at the time. However, later on, when that second home can stand alone without comparison to the more elegant one, it may turn out to be just right for you and your wallet.

Keep Sellers' Home Description Sheets

These days almost all sellers will offer buyers a single sheet of paper that has a picture of the home along with the most important facts about it, such as price, size, number of bedrooms and baths, and special features. Each time you are shown a home, chances are one of these sheets will be there.

Take and save these home description sheets. Many savvy buyers obtain a small folder or notebook to accumulate and save the sheets. They even code the sheets to corresponding locations on their real estate map.

Later on, after you've forgotten all but the skimpiest of details about the property, the sheet will help prod your memory. It will take you back to the property and let you mentally walk through it. Combined with the map, which shows the location of the property, these sheets are a thorough and useful way to keep track of all the ground you've covered when house hunting.

Get to Know the Market as Quickly as Possible

The map (and home description sheets) provide an additional function. They quickly get you up and running as to what the real estate market is really like at the moment you're looking.

For example, after only a single day of house hunting and after seeing only about half a dozen homes, you should already be forming a strong opinion of what's available in certain areas and at what price. If you've marked off the homes you've seen on your map, and kept the description sheets, you should be able to say that within a certain neighborhood, there's a home of a certain type selling for $200,000. Now you know not only about the home, but about those similar to it in its area.

Go out a few times to narrow your search by eliminating certain neighborhoods and concentrating on others. You may find that you like a certain type of home and its price range and want to see other homes in the same area, thus further narrowing your search. In this manner, you can in short order get up to speed on market conditions.

It doesn't matter if you fail to make an offer on any of the houses that you've seen. In the early phase of house hunting, you're really just educating yourself on the market so that you'll be able to recognize a good deal when you spot it. It's sort of like shopping for a car. Until you've seen all the models and brands in your price range, you really can't make an intelligent decision on which one is best for you. Similarly, until you've seen the homes that are available, how can you know which is best for you—which is a really good deal?

Power Tip 10
Build a Plan of Action

There are two ways to accomplish almost anything. One method is to simply jump in and thrash around, hoping that eventually you blunder into your goal. The second is to anticipate the steps you'll need to take to reach your goal and then create a plan of action to get you there. The first method is hit or miss, something that children often do before they've learned how to succeed at tasks. The second is what *you'll* do because you want to be organized and in control and, most important of all, want to get the best home deal possible.

In order to create an action plan that will result in getting the house of your dreams at a price you consider reasonable, you need to first answer three basic questions. Don't make any offers on homes until you've addressed these three.

Questions You Must Answer

1. How Much Can You Afford to Pay for a Home? There's no point in going to Tiffany if you can only afford K-Mart. It will just be a frustrating experience. Similarly, why look at homes that cost $500,000 (except out of curiosity) when your pocketbook limits you to homes in a lower range?

If you're not sure how much you can afford, go back to the second Power Tip and check it out. It explains how to find a lender and get preapproved. Preapproval will let you know how much you can afford so that you can look for homes in your price range. It's one of the most important steps to take when house hunting.

Be aware that what a lender says you can afford may not be what you feel comfortable with. You may feel better paying less—or more. You can always take out a smaller mortgage. And there are creative financing techniques to get you into a much more expensive house than lenders say you can handle, if that's the course you want to take. (See Chapter 5, on working with lenders.)

2. Where Do You Want to Buy?   We live in a vast country filled with homes, close to 70 million at last count. You can live in the desert, on the water, in the mountains—the sky's the limit.

No, not really. Very few of us have that much freedom in deciding where we want to live. Rather, we must find a place close to our work, perhaps close to family and friends, in a climate that we find hospitable (in case we have allergies or illness), and so on. (It's only with a second home that many people find true freedom of living choice, but that's another story!)

Even within a geographic area limited by where we work, there will always be choices. As we've seen, you'll undoubtedly want a neighborhood with good schools, low crime, good transportation, nearby shopping, and so on. But you probably won't be able to get it all. There will be trade-offs, often between housing price and the quality of the neighborhood. Let's face it, the best neighborhoods cost the most. Many times we simply have to settle for second best, or even third.

Then there's the matter of whether you want to live in a single-family detached house, essentially your own castle, or in a shared home such as a condo, townhouse, or co-op. There are pluses and minuses for each and, again, trade-offs in terms of price. Usually, but not always, shared housing costs substantially less than single-family units.

As part of your home-buying process, you should become familiar with different neighborhoods as well as the different types of home ownership available. Expose yourself to your options. You may find that there's something out there you really like, that's affordable, but that you never before considered.

3. What Kind of Market Are You In?   Finally, you need to ask yourself what kind of market conditions you are buying into. In real estate there are three kinds of markets: hot, normal, and cold.

Hot.   A hot market, such as we've had in recent years, means that there are more buyers chasing fewer homes. As a result, homes will sell often as soon as they are listed (sometimes before the listing even comes out!). There may be multiple offers on each home from buyers competing to purchase. And the homes may even sell for more than their asking price. In this market housing prices are accelerating upward, so if you want to be a player, you must have all your ducks in a row and be able to act quickly.

Normal. A normal market finds a fairly large inventory of homes for sale. In the industry inventory is measured by how long it takes to sell the average home. A sale time of 60 to 120 days is usually considered normal. In this type of market, you don't need to rush to find a home or make desperate offers. Of course, there are other buyers about, so you need to move as quickly as possible on a home you want. But you can expect to make offers at lower than the asking price and eventually negotiate a price at least somewhat less than what the sellers are asking.

Cold. A cold market is what real estate experienced from the end of the 1980s into the middle 1990s. Homes were listed for a year or more without any offers. Prices were falling, in some areas as much as 30 to 40 percent off their previous highs. There was a huge inventory of unsold homes and almost no buyers.

In this type of market, you can take your time making an offer. You can leisurely look at property. And most certainly you will want to low-ball any offers—in fact, make them for much less than the sellers are asking. Because of the possibility of future drops in price (it's very hard to know when the bottom will be reached), you'll want to try to keep ahead of the market and buy for as low as possible. Sellers will know this and will be as accommodating as they can. After all, that's the only way they can get out. Expect to find many repossessions offered for sale by banks and others. It's a great time to be a buyer, a terrible time to be a seller.

You can get information on the housing inventory and the time to sell a home from any real estate agent. You can also ask how common multiple offers are, whether homes are selling for more than their asking price, and whether repos are available. If your agent can't help you, contact the local real estate board. Much of the information is also available on the Web (www.dataquick.com, home-pricecheck.com, homeadvisor.com). Also check articles in local newspapers and simply ask lenders how the market's doing. It won't take you long to discover where things stand.

Once you've identified the market, you will know how to act. Throughout this book you'll see different tactics and strategies to use depending on market conditions.

Plan Your Action

Once you've answered the three questions, you can plan the steps to take to find the home of your dreams at an affordable price. Find an agent with whom you feel comfortable working and then start looking. When making an offer, always use tactics appropriate to market conditions. Here are the steps to take. You fill in the blanks.

STEP 1: Get Preapproval

Lender's name _____

Lender's phone _____

Lender's Web site/e-mail address _____

_____

Lender's physical address _____

_____

STEP 2: Decide Where You Want to Live _____

Neighborhood 1: _____

Distance to work _____ miles _____ minutes

During rush hour _____ miles _____ minutes

School percentiles _____

Graffiti Index (crime rate)   high_____ avg._____ low_____

Distance to shopping _____ miles _____ minutes

Distance to transportation _____ miles _____ minutes

Homes you could live in available?   Yes [ ] No [ ]

Neighborhood 2: _____

Distance to work _____ miles _____ minutes

During rush hour _____ miles _____ minutes

School percentiles _____

Graffiti Index (crime rate)   high_____ avg._____ low_____

Distance to shopping _____ miles _____ minutes

Distance to transportation _____ miles _____ minutes

Homes you could live in available?   Yes [ ] No [ ]

Neighborhood 3: _____

Distance to work _____ miles _____ minutes

During rush hour _____ miles _____ minutes

School percentiles _____

Graffiti Index (crime rate)   high_____ avg._____ low_____

Distance to shopping _____ miles _____ minutes

Distance to transportation _____ miles _____ minutes

Homes you could live in available?   Yes [ ] No [ ]

STEP 3: Discover the Market's Condition

Average time to sell a home: 30 days_____ 60 days_____

90 days_____120 days_____6 months_____ longer_____

Multiple offers common? Yes [ ] No [ ]

Houses selling for more than asking price? Yes [ ] No [ ]

Houses selling for less than asking price? Yes [ ] No [ ]

Lots of repos on the market? Yes [ ] No [ ]

STEP 4: Get an Agent

Have you found one agent who feels comfortable? Yes [ ] No [ ]

Have you tried a buyer's agent? Yes [ ] No [ ]

STEP 5: Begin Looking

Are you going out almost every weekend? Yes [ ] No [ ]

Are you ready to act quickly in a hot market? Yes [ ] No [ ]

Are you prepared to offer more than the asking price to get your home in a hot market? Yes [ ] No [ ]

Is the market condition normal? Yes [ ] No [ ]

If the market's cold, have you looked for repos? Yes [ ] No [ ]

Are you prepared to come in with a very low-ball offer in a cold market? Yes [ ] No [ ]

See the checklist for *Plan Before You Purchase* on page 204.

2
Strategies for a Hot Market

Power Tip 11
Do Your Own Canvassing
in a Hot Market

The market's tight, you've been looking for months, and you can't find a home to buy. What can you do? Try canvassing a few neighborhoods.

Agents call it "farming." They will pick out an area and get to know it very well, often calling themselves specialists in that part of town. On a regular basis they will come by and talk to the people living there, dropping off their card. They will send out flyers, calendars, and notices of homes sold. The idea is that when people in the area decide to sell and look around for an agent, they will come to the "farmer." It works surprisingly well.

In a sizzling hot market when homes are scarce, you can do the same thing. If you go door to door and let people know that you're in the market to buy a home, sometimes you can connect with sellers before they list their property. If you can save the sellers at least part of the commission, they will be very happy to accept an offer from you. When the market's hot and it's hard to find houses, canvassing can be a great way to get a home for yourself, often at a lower than market price (your half of the commission is saved).

Be aware, however, that canvassing (or farming) is time-intensive. Unless you're willing to go door to door, you might miss the one home that's ready to come onto the market.

Whenever I canvas, I print up a little card explaining to potential sellers that I am a principal (a buyer looking for a home, not an agent looking to list) and am interested in immediately buying a home such as theirs. I then ask the sellers, if they are interested, to call me at the number on the card. I've gotten many calls back.

Although you can hire someone to distribute the cards, that's not usually a good idea. The reason is that when you do it yourself, you stand a good chance of meeting the owners at home. You can strike up a conversation and if they're not selling their home, they may know of someone in the neighborhood who is. Now you can go see that person and say a neighbor recommended you; you've definitely got the inside track.

Beware of walking some neighborhoods. We live in an age where street crime can be violent and there is always the possibility you could be a victim. Of course, you won't want to buy into such a neighborhood. Nevertheless, it's always better to go out in twos, rather than alone, and during daylight hours instead of after dark.

What Do I Do When I Find a Seller?

Your best or worst day may be when you find someone who's actually ready to sell. What do you do then?

If you're experienced in real estate, you whip out your purchase agreement and begin writing up an offer. If not, you begin by negotiating with the seller not only over price and terms, but also over an agent to handle the paperwork. And decide who will pay the costs.

Often, if buyer and seller have found each other and have agreed in principle on a sale, an agent will handle the paperwork for a fee. Some agents, of course, will still insist on a full commission. Others may want half a commission. Still others may agree to, say, a few thousand dollars.

You should be aware that there are real estate lawyers, particularly in parts of the East Coast, who regularly handle home transactions for ridiculously low fees, often just $500 or $1,000. One of these may be willing to handle the paperwork of the transaction as well. And fee-for-service brokers are growing at a rapid rate.

In a hot market, once you find sellers who are willing to deal exclusively with you, don't let them go. Do whatever it takes to keep them happy and to get a purchase for yourself.

Power Tip 12
Find the One Agent
Who Can Deliver

Sometimes it's necessary to go through several agents before you find the right one, the agent who can deliver the property you want. The trouble is, it can take a lot of time to discover that the agent you're currently working with isn't the right one for you.

Agents value loyalty in their clients almost above everything else. Stories are rampant in the trade about disloyal buyers who work with an agent for months and then, when it came time to buy, submit an offer through a different agent. (The agent left out usually gets nothing for his or her efforts.) If you find a productive agent, stick with him or her. Loyalty works both ways.

If the market is sizzling hot, you may need to be perfectly clear with your agent. If an agent waits until homes come out on the multiple listing service before showing them to you, and then you discover they're already sold before you even can make an offer, it's time for drastic action. Explain that you want and need a home in this market and you can't really wait for it to be listed on the multiple. You need to get in earlier.

You may even need to say that you'll no longer work with that agent, but instead plan to look elsewhere. You'll give your name to other agents, especially those who are "listers," in the hopes of learning about the houses early. (A lister is an agent who specializes in listing homes, as opposed to working with both buyers and sellers.) Listing agents may be able to let you know of a home that has just come on the market, so you can get your offer in early.

Of course, if you have a favorite agent, you will want to stick with that person if possible. But if that agent can't find you a house, and another agent can, what choice do you have? You have to say, "Sorry, but I want a home and if this is what it takes to get it, then so be it."

In many areas the agent who first shows you the property may be entitled to a commission, even if you later buy through another agent. To avoid hard feelings and split commissions (and potential legal entanglements), many agents won't show you homes you've previously seen with other agents, unless a reasonable time has passed—usually more than a month.

Do Other Agents Really Have Better Homes to Show?

Not "better" homes, but other homes. Agents who belong to multiple services usually are supposed to list all homes with the service and make them available to all other agents as soon as possible. In a hot market, however, listers who normally put everything on the multiple may hold the listing off for several days or a week before letting other brokers know about it. In the trade, this is called a "vest pocket listing" and is considered unethical behavior.

Do vest pocket listings exist? Of course they do, particularly when the market is hot and the lister feels that all it takes is a few days with no competition from other agents to find a buyer. (An agent who finds both buyer and seller avoids having to split the commission.)

In addition, some agents do not cobroke all the properties they list. That means that they don't allow other agents to work on all their listings. They have exclusives, which only they work on. Although this is not to the benefit of the seller, if the agent tells the seller and the seller agrees, it's certainly not illegal. Thus sometimes there are homes for sale that are between FSBOs (for sale by owner) and multiple listings; these homes are in a sort of gray area that only one agent is working on. Unless you're working with that agent, you won't know about the property.

Thus, by making your interests known to a great many agents, particularly listers, you may one day get a call saying that if you can act within the next two hours, you'll have the inside track on a newly listed home. When homes are selling fast and furious, it may be one of your best options.

Countering the advantages of using several agents is the confidence factor of working with a single good one. If you work with one agent exclusively, one you trust, that agent can be extremely helpful in coaching you on making offers and good deals. For example, the agent may be able to ferret out when the seller is desperate and will take less. Or in a sizzling market, the agent may suggest that in order to get the property you should offer *more* than the asking price (as well as how much more). In deep waters such as these, a trusted adviser can be an invaluable asset.

Power Tip 13
Track Down Elusive Sellers

Your offer can't be accepted unless and until the sellers see it. However, surprising as it may seem, in a hot market finding the sellers in order to present an offer can be a difficult and tricky thing, especially when sellers have a good chance, just by waiting, of obtaining multiple offers.

It's vital to recognize that you're always in competition with other buyers for any property. In an average or a cool market, it's unusual for a seller to get more than one offer at a time. Instead, things usually happen in an orderly fashion. You write out an offer and give it to your agent, who then calls the seller's agent. At a convenient time, usually that day, both agents meet with the seller, who then decides whether to accept, reject, or counter your offer.

However, when the market is sizzling hot and sellers know that there's the possibility of multiple offers, they sometimes "bug out." By that I mean they become unavailable. They may tell their agent something like, "We're going out of town for three weeks and can't be reached. We'll call you when we get back."

When You've Got the Inside Track

Now consider this scenario. You've been searching and searching for a home you like and can afford. But every time you find one, you're the proverbial "day late and a dollar short." Someone else has already submitted an offer that's been accepted (or there are multiple offers), and you lose out.

One day, thanks to your perseverance, you track down a home that's just come onto the market. You manage to get in to see it by coming around just as a cleaning crew is leaving—you sneak in. It's perfect for you. What's more, since the house is locked up after you, you're pretty sure not only that you are the first one in to see it, but that it will be another day before anyone else gets in to see it. You've got the inside track.

By now you're quite sure that as soon as other buyers out there see the home, there will be additional offers. So you have your agent immediately draw up the offer (probably full price) and allow only until midnight for the sellers to accept. Hopefully the sellers will have to decide on your offer immediately, before others have a chance to submit theirs.

However, late that afternoon your agent reports back that she's contacted the seller's agent only to discover that the sellers are going to be out of town for a week or so. The seller's agent suggests you extend the time period for acceptance and your offer will be presented when the sellers get back.

Not a chance, you tell yourself. In a week there could be a half dozen or more other offers. And you know that the offers are presented all together, not in the order submitted. Chances are someone will present a better offer than yours (perhaps over full price) and you'll lose out again. What can you do?

One Solution—Wait Out the Sellers

One agent I know who found his buyers in this situation decided to take matters into his own hands. When he was told that the sellers were out of town for a week, he reasoned that this was most unlikely. After all, why would sellers put their home up for sale and then leave town? More likely, they were just bugging out until a stack of offers appeared, so that they could then pit one buyer against another and get a better deal.

So the agent camped out across the street from the sellers' home. Sure enough, around eight at night, the sellers drove up. He immediately went over, introduced himself, and told the sellers that he had an offer he'd like to present.

The sellers were astounded and protested that it was late and, besides, they wanted their agent present.

Never too late to make a deal, the agent told them. Then, using his cell phone, he called the other agent and told her to get right down there. Needless to say, the other agent was as upset as the sellers. Still, not wanting to let anything get past her, she managed to get to their home in 20 minutes. Now all the necessary parties were there. The agent representing the buyers had an offer expiring at midnight, and he presented it.

It was a good offer, cash to the sellers for full price. (The buyers, of course, were getting a new mortgage, but had an unconditional preapproval letter.) A cash deal to the sellers, exactly what they had asked for in their listing. A slam dunk, right?

Wrong. The sellers protested. This wasn't at all what they had in mind. They wanted to wait for other offers to come in. Perhaps someone would offer them more than they were asking. They wanted to wait and see. They wouldn't accept this offer. They had been hoodwinked!

The intrepid agent representing the buyers looked at the bleary-eyed seller's agent, who looked back. They both nodded, then proceeded to explain the facts of life to the sellers.

No, they most certainly did not need to accept this offer. Indeed, no one would force them to sell their house. However, they had signed a listing agreement that specified a price and terms. According to the listing agreement, no sale was required for the agent to earn a commission. The only requirement was that a buyer be presented who was Ready, Willing, and Able to purchase under the terms specified in the listing. That had been done. So, if the sellers decided not to sell, as they well could, they still owed a full commission.

The sellers were outraged and ranted at their agent. They said it was unfair and threatened to call their lawyer. Their agent backed down and said it was just a formality. She wanted to see her sellers happy and would certainly not hold them to her share of the listing commission. (Why should she when she was certain of a sale within a few days one way or another?)

The agent representing the buyers, however, was less considerate. As a subagent of the sellers, he felt he was entitled to his commission, having gone the extra yard to earn it. He wasn't backing down.

The sellers fumed and fussed. Eventually, however, when it was pointed out that they weren't losing anything, since the offer on the table in any event was for their asking price, and there was no guarantee or higher offers coming in, they reluctantly signed. The agent had a deal—and so did his buyers.

Will your agent go the extra yard? I certainly hope so. If not, you should consider getting a better agent.

The rule here is that persistence pays off. It's rare that sellers will list their house and then actually leave town. Most are just hiding out in a hot market waiting for those multiple offers. Find and confront them, either directly or through an agent, and you could get a signed deal.

Note: In common practice an agent presenting an offer goes through the listing agent and does not contact the sellers directly. However, in an extreme market, some extremely unusual things do happen.

Power Tip 14
Offer More Than the
Asking Price

If offering more than the asking price goes against your grain, don't feel bad. Most buyers feel it's not only absurd, it's downright insulting. It's sort of like going to a supermarket to buy a jar of mustard and demanding that the checkout attendant let you pay more than the amount rung up on the cash register. Who would do such a thing, participate in such nonsense?

A desperate buyer would, in a sizzling hot market, that's who!

It happened in parts of the East Coast at the end of the 1980s. It happened again with a vengeance in California, espescially around Silicon Valley, at the turn of the century. In the decade in between there was a deep real estate recession. But whenever the economy is booming, a buying frenzy can happen. Perhaps it's occurring in your area as you read this. If you compare the demographics of most parts of the country with the inventory of housing, you very quickly see that in many markets, particularly along the coasts, there is an imbalance. More people want homes than there are homes available. And when prices begin to move up and people can't find homes, it turns into a buying frenzy that forces prices higher, with offers for more than a home's asking price. (Not long ago I observed a multiple offer sale in which the winning buyer paid over $50,000 more than the asking price for a $450,000 home—that must be some kind of record!)

Even if you've never before been in this kind of market, you'll recognize it immediately. You want a home, but there simply aren't many up for grabs. When you finally do find one and make an offer, you discover that someone else has either beaten you there or offered more than you did, sometimes more than the seller was asking.

What Are the Rules?

As they say in the B movies, there aren't any rules. Or at least you have to make them up as you go. What's important is to get a good understanding of what's happening.

When the market's tight, the competition for homes is ferocious. In a normal market, you see a house, you like it, and you make an offer, usually for less than the asking price. The agents sit down with the sellers and try to convince them to accept your offer. Sometimes the sellers do; sometimes they don't. If they don't, you're at least likely to get a counteroffer, somewhere above what you offered, but below the asking price.

In a sizzling hot market, however, things are different. You tour a home and as you're walking through it, half a dozen other buyers are coming through. Often as you leave, you see one or more of them writing up an offer with their agents.

You like the place, so you decide to make an offer. Your agent calls the seller's agent to explain that she has an offer coming in. This is a courtesy that helps alert the seller's agent to be available. As another courtesy, the seller's agent may also alert the seller to be available to receive an offer.

Only when your agent comes back do you learn that half a dozen other agents have also called, all of them saying they anticipate bringing in offers. Suddenly you realize that it's a crowded playing field.

Your agent tells you that your best chance of getting the home, perhaps your only chance, is to present your best offer first. Never mind about low balling. Never mind about cutting 5 percent off the asking price to see if you can get it for less. You now have to convince the seller that your offer is better than any others.

So you tell your agent you don't want to fool around with this game. You'll simply offer what the seller is asking. You'll close out the other bidders.

Your agent shakes her head and says that from what she's seen the past few months, the other buyers are thinking the same way. If you really want to get this house, you'd better offer *more* than the seller is asking. Suddenly you're in a fast race whose outcome you can't predict. Furthermore, in order to run, you have to be willing to dash blindly toward the finish line.

How much more to offer? If you offer $1,000 more and the others offer $10,000, you lose the home. On the other hand, if you offer $10,000 and the others don't offer more, or offer only $1,000 more, you still lose by paying too much. And what is the house really worth? What can you do?

Just as there are no rules, there are no answers when playing this game.

My suggestion is that you never offer more than you think the house is worth, no matter what the competition is doing. It may just be that all the competitors are offering too much. It's better to wait until the market cools down a bit. And, it will.

On the other hand, you may feel that the market is so hot and prices are moving up so rapidly that a higher bid is warranted. If that's the case, make your best bid and don't regret it.

Finally, if it turns out that someone has outbid you, avoid getting into a bidding war (described next). Usually the only person to win there is the seller.

Power Tip 15
Avoid Multiple Offers

In a normal market, if two offers are made simultaneously on a single home, the agent with the lesser offer will often ask for a break in negotiations with the seller to consult his buyer. He'll then call and explain that there's another offer, perhaps better. If you want the home, he'll try to stall (while the agent representing the other buyer tries to force closure) to give you time to up your ante.

This approach doesn't really work well because it's hard to write a new offer in the heat of battle, particularly when the sellers are already considering a better one than you previously made.

One solution, as noted in the last Power Tip, is to simply make your highest possible offer and hope for the best. Yes, if the other offers are much lower, you could pay more than you should for the property. On the other hand, in a sizzling market you're probably hoping to get in at any price.

Give Your Agent the Option of
Deciding the Price You'll Pay

This strategy requires that you have total faith in the integrity of your agent and that he or she is solely a buyer's agent—that is, representing you, not the seller. Having this kind of faith in your agent normally comes only when you've been working with the same agent for a long time, often through previous deals.

You know (or believe) that there will be other offers on the property, probably for more money. So, since you won't be there when the offers are presented, you authorize your agent to up your offer as needed to beat out the other offers—up to a certain maximum amount. Any smart agent will insist that you put this into writing.

The strategy is fraught with dangers. An unprincipled agent could simply walk in and make your highest offer, thus not only immediately winning the bidding (perhaps), but also ensuring a higher commission. (Remember, the commission is based on the sales price.)

When the Seller Responds with Multiple Counteroffers

On the other hand, when there are multiple offers on a property, the seller may reject them all and instead make multiple counter offers. What's a multiple counteroffer? That's a good question. My own take is that it's not really a legitimate counteroffer to you at all. Rather, it's an invitation to you to up your offer.

> Offers must be presented to the seller as they come in. The seller must be allowed to consider all of them. It's not a case where the seller considers the first offer to come in and then either accepts or rejects it before going to the next offer. All offers are presented as they come in, even if that means simultaneously, and the seller can pick and choose at will.

With a multiple counteroffer, the seller will typically write out an offer at a desired price with the most favorable terms (usually cash) to the seller and relatively few contingencies (sometimes none at all) to protect you. The implication is that if you want the property, you must sign the offer as the seller has presented it.

The problem, however, is that the seller may make the same or a different offer to more than just you. So-called multiple counter offers may be extended to half a dozen would-be buyers.

As a result, even if you sign the offer exactly as agreed, there's no guarantee that you have bought the property. A multiple counter offer usually includes a clause stating that the counteroffer is not valid until the seller has countersigned your signature and let you know that fact. The deal isn't made until the seller has accepted your acceptance of the counteroffer!

> In any true offer or counteroffer, it takes only the signature of the other party and transmittal of that fact to the person making the offer to create a valid deal. For example, if you offer to buy a property and the seller signs your offer and then transmits that information to you, you have a deal. Similarly, if you sign a normal counteroffer and then transmit that information to the seller, there's a deal. Not so with multiple counteroffers.

The multiple counteroffer will also contain a clause stating specifically that the seller is countering to one or more buyers at the same or different price and terms and that this multiple counteroffer is not binding unless and until it is signed again by the seller, with that information transmitted to you. (The reason the information of the signature has to be transmitted to you is that, technically speaking, you could withdraw your offer any time before you are informed that the seller has signed.)

What, then, is a multiple counteroffer? As noted, to my way of thinking it is an offer to rebid on the property at terms specified by the seller. It doesn't lock the seller in to you. On the other hand, if you sign, it locks you in.

Should You Go Along with a Multiple Counteroffer?

Don't sign unless you absolutely must have the property. My advice is to bow out and let others fight over the bones. The market will eventually cool and there will be other homes. Eventually you may get an even better deal somewhere. Just remember, the multiple counteroffer mostly benefits the seller.

On the other hand, if this is the only property you'll ever be happy with, then sign the multiple counteroffer. To increase your chances of securing it, you may even want to up the ante and offer more than the seller is asking—to beat out other would-be buyers!

In a normal offer or counteroffer, time is of the essence. You'll want an answer immediately, usually in no more than 24 hours. (We'll discuss why in a later Power Tip.) In a multiple counteroffer, however, there is usually a relaxed time for acceptance, often two to three days. After all, why should the seller hurry things along? The more the seller waits, the more offers are likely to come in—at higher prices.

A multiple counteroffer is really just a tool for a bidding war. It's one of those games where often the best way to win is not to play.

Power Tip 16
Get Your Offer in Early
Before Others Arrive

The adage that the early bird gets the worm applies here. If you wait in a hot market, chances are that one of two things will happen. By the time you get ready to submit your offer, other buyers will be ready with theirs and it will devolve into a competition, in which case you lose one way or another. Or another buyer will beat you to the punch and the property will already be sold by the time you get there. All of which is to say that if you want to get a home in a sizzling market, you must be ready to act instantly.

What does acting instantly mean? It means that as soon as you locate a home that's potentially right for you, make an offer. Don't hesitate. Don't wait around to consider it for another day, or for another walk-through. Act immediately.

Of course, in order to act quickly, you must have all your ducks in a row. At a minimum:

- Have a preapproval letter ready to go.

- Have the money ready to move into your checking account so you can confidently write out a deposit check.

- Have the money ready for the down payment and closing costs so you can close the deal within the time constraints.

- Be familiar with the purchase agreement so you understand it and can fill it out quickly without having to spend a lot of time asking questions or taking it to your attorney.

- Know the market so you can immediately tell what the value of the property should be.

- Have an agent waiting in the wings to prepare and present an offer for you.

When the market's hot, you have to be quick on your feet; otherwise the property you want will always get away.

Power Tip 17
Buy Sight Unseen

Buy a property before you even see it? Anyone who would do that must be daft! Talk about buying a pig in a poke. Here you might be buying a horse only to find out it's a chicken!

While it does seem rather extreme to make an offer on a property you've never seen, consider this situation. A couple wants to purchase a condominium. They have been looking for several months. However, the market is so hot that by the time they get out to see properties they might like, the good ones are already sold. It's a case of always being a day late.

Then, one day an agent calls at 9 in the morning and says, "I've found the perfect place for you. It's the right size, in a good location, and the price is what you want to pay. Only you'll have to act quickly to get it. I've already called the sellers and told them I will present the offer within the hour. Can you get down here to sign and give me the deposit check?"

Yes, of course. The buyers just barely have time to do that. But there's no time to see the property. Nevertheless, they go ahead and make the offer. And the sellers accept. Now the buyers have a fine home, which they sheepishly ask if they can see the next day.

Never Really Buy Before You See the Property?

This rule is as old as real estate. The reason is that no two properties are exactly alike. You can't possibly know if you're going to like what you're buying unless you see it. That usually means not just one quick glance, but coming back a couple of times to check it out.

Does this advice fly in the face of our example above, which suggests that in a superhot market it might be necessary to buy before looking? Yes and no.

Some desperate buyers have found a way of tying up the property in a purchase and then getting in to see it later. If they don't like what they see, they then back out of the deal. It's sort of like having your cake and eating it too.

Guerilla Purchasing Tactics

Savvy buyers know that in today's market, a sale isn't a sale until all the contingencies have been removed. The two biggest are disclosures (automatic in most states) and a home inspection. In a properly drawn purchase agreement, the buyers have the right to back out and get their deposit returned if they don't approve of either the sellers' disclosures or the inspection report.

Don't like what the sellers say are defects in the property? You're out. Don't like what the inspection report discloses? The deal's finished.

The purpose of these "outs," of course, is to allow the buyers to really examine the property to see if its value is as initially presented by the sellers. It's a tool to ensure that buyers aren't getting stuck with defective properties.

But some buyers, faced with the difficulty of purchasing a home in a supertight market, have stretched the envelope. They now use the "outs" to tie down the property so they can examine it at their leisure to determine whether it's for them.

In California, for example, buyers have an automatic three days to back out after they see the sellers' disclosures. The clock doesn't start running until they receive and sign for those disclosures.

So some desperate California buyers send in purchase offers sight unseen on properties they think they will like. If they are the successful buyers, they then have three days to get in there and examine not only the disclosures but the property itself. If they decide they really don't want it, they simply disapprove of the disclosures, and they're out.

The Perils of Sight Unseen

While this tactic may work, it can also backfire. What happens, for example, if the sellers disclose no defects whatsoever? What if the inspection report (which some buyers also use as a backdoor exit) turns up nothing wrong with the property? Can the buyers still disapprove of the disclosures or inspection report and get out of the deal gracefully?

In the case where approval, regardless of what the report shows, is a statutory requirement (as in those states with strict disclosure laws), the answer is probably yes. If the law requires approval and the buyers disapprove, there should be no deal.

On the other hand, when the right to approve a disclosure statement or an inspection report is not statutory but only written into a contract as a contingency, the area turns gray. The sellers might claim foul if the buyers disapprove both documents.

Indeed, some seller's agents have taken to writing into the contingency that the right of disapproval hinges on the finding of "substantial defects" in the property. Of course, the buyers could refuse to go along with that (and possibly lose out on the property in a hot market). Even if they do, however, the argument now becomes one of what's substantial, and that's another can of worms. However, if *no* defects are found, then the buyers could be in trouble.

> It's rare for an inspection to report no defects. Almost always something turns up, even if it's just a broken electrical plug or a leaking faucet. However, sellers who are anxious to get rid of their property will frequently simply say they know of no defects in their disclosures.

"But I Like the Property!"

There is always the possibility that buying sight unseen will result in getting a property you really like. This is particularly the case with buyers who have been shopping for some time and are purchasing in an area of similar homes—for example, condominiums. I have known buyers who simply fall in love with a particular condo development. They say, "I just want one of those. I don't care which one. Just let me buy it."

In this case, buying sight unseen works well. It yields the buyers the home of their dreams in a market where taking the time to look thoroughly might have caused them to lose out.

Power Tip 18
Look for "As Is" Homes

Occasionally in a hot market you can wring a good deal out of sellers who have a problem property. Because the sellers don't want to fix the problem, they have to lower their price. Often these homes sell for substantially less than neighboring property, providing you with a rare opportunity to get in low.

How do you find a problem property? Look for properties for sale on an "as is" basis.

What Does "As Is" Really Mean?

Normally there's an implied warranty that goes with the sale. It's that the sellers will fix up the property so that it's in good shape when sold. In other words, they will get rid of any problems. For example, if you discover that there's mold growing on a wall, they'll get rid of the mold and repaint the wall. If the water heater's bad, they'll fix it. If there are more serious problems requiring a more costly fix, such as a roof replacement, they'll negotiate with you over the price, but will generally fund most of the cost.

However, when the house is sold "as is," the sellers are letting you know that they won't do anything to fix it up. You have to take it just like it is—moldy walls, leaky roof, and anything else that might be wrong.

Most buyers, however, are loath to do that. They don't want problems; they want everything solved. When they move in, they want the property to be ready to go. As a consequence, in order to attract buyers, homes sold "as is" almost always command a lower price. You can make an offer on this kind of home and, even in a sizzling market, hope to get it for below what the sellers are asking.

I recently bought a home "as is" in a market where houses were sold within days of being listed and where multiple offers were common. The "as is" house, however, had been on the market for nearly three months and the seller, a relocation company, was dropping the price $10,000 a week in the hope of finding a buyer. I found the house to be a great bargain.

What About the Problem With the Home?

The rub, of course, is that you not only get the house; you usually also get a problem. It's up to you to identify the problem, determine if you can correct it, and then find out how much the correction will cost.

> Be aware that buying a house "as is" does not free the seller from having to give full disclosure. Nor does it take away your right to inspect the home fully. The usual rules still apply.

This means that you will want to do two things: (1) read the disclosures very closely, and (2) have the most thorough inspection possible. You want to find out what's so wrong with the property that the sellers are willing to go "as is" and accept a lower price.

What are some of the likely problems? Here's a partial list, starting with the most serious:

- Severe neighborhood negative (e.g., close to toxic dump site, next to all-night liquor store)
- Degrading soil (e.g., house slipping down hillside, partially under water, leaking radon or methane gas in soil)
- Cracked foundation
- Structural faults
- Leaking roof
- Bad plumbing, electrical, heating, or air-conditioning system
- Broken driveway, fences, or windows
- Cosmetic damage (e.g., needs paint, wallpaper, carpeting)
- Virtually nothing at all wrong

Obviously, if the home has a severe problem, you're going to want not only to clearly define it but also to come up with the cost of a solution. A new roof could easily cost $10,000 or more. A cracked foundation could cost $25,000 or more. Degraded soil might not be fixable at any cost. And there's little you can do about a neighborhood negative. On the other hand, if all the house needs is some paint and new carpeting, you might very easily be able to handle that. You'll want to adjust your offer to take into account your cost of fixing up.

Some Houses Sold "As Is" Don't Have Any Real Problem

Note that on the list above, the very bottom problem is "nothing at all wrong." Why should sellers go "as is" if there is nothing at all wrong with the property?

There are lots of reasons. In the case of the property I recently bought, noted above, the relocation company simply didn't want to be bothered with fixing up anything. The company was interested in a quick, clean sale.

However, potential buyers were put off by the fact that the disclosures revealed no defects. They assumed that the seller was hiding something, and hence shied away. On the other hand, when my inspection revealed no problems, I eagerly moved forward. The relocation company was glad to be rid of the property, and it was a great deal for me.

Sellers sometimes sell "as is" under the mistaken belief that doing so relieves them of any liability if the buyers discover a problem with the property. Remember, selling "as is" does not normally free the sellers from disclosure. The sellers must still disclose any serious problems of which they are aware. Selling "as is" means only that after the sellers disclose all problems, they won't be responsible for fixing them.

Not long ago a broker in a nearby community advised all the sellers of properties he had listed to sell "as is," so they could avoid potential lawsuits after the sale from buyers who discovered defects that the sellers should have known about, but didn't reveal. When I suggested to him that this was a poor strategy, he said he had recently been sued successfully by an angry buyer and was determined to protect himself and his clients. I noted that a better strategy was to have the sellers reveal everything and to insist that the buyers conduct a thorough inspection.

When you buy "as is" you need to do more than just have an inspector stop by for an hour or two and glance at the property. You need to have a good inspector take the time to look in normally hidden areas such as in the attic, under the house, and under the wall-to-wall carpeting—even to the point of checking the foundation foot by foot. Structural and soils reports would also not be a bad idea. (Be sure to get the sellers' permission for more thorough checks, which might soil or damage the property.)

How Do You Know How Much to Offer?

Follow these key steps to buying a house "as is":

1. Identify the problem.

2. Determine how much it will cost to fix it up to your standards. (You might be willing to live with bad paint and only clean the carpets, at least for a while.) Subtract the cost from the market value.

3. Determine the nuisance value of having to fix up the property and subtract this cost from the market value.

4. Judge how motivated the sellers are and how difficult it's been for them to sell, then lower your offer even further.

5. Make your "as is" offer and stick to it.

What If You Discover a Problem Later On?

As with any other home purchase, any undiscovered problem becomes yours. It's your headache *unless* you feel that the problem existed before you bought and the sellers knew (or should have known) about it and failed to disclose it to you. If the latter is the case, you will certainly want to go back to the sellers to ask that they pay to have the problem fixed.

Power Tip 19
Look for Fixer-Uppers

A fixer-upper is a home that has been trashed or rundown. (On the East Coast it's sometimes called a "handyman's special.") Often it was a rental. Sometimes it was left vacant and vandalized. Many times the home looks terrible. A typical fixer-upper might have heavily soiled and worn carpeting, broken windows, dirty walls, and broken appliances and fixtures. Another type of fixer-upper is a home with a problem such as a cracked slab or foundation, weathered doors and window frames, or even something as simple as poor paint.

The idea with a fixer-upper is that you get a discounted price because of the things wrong with the property. Then, often using your own dollars and sweat, you fix up the home and either live in it or resell for a sometimes healthy profit.

> Fixer-uppers are usually, but not always, sold "as is." (See the last Power Tip.) Very often the sellers simply want out quickly and aren't willing to spend the money and time to fix the place up.

A Heavily Discounted Price

In order for a home to sell at top dollar, it must look good. When potential buyers walk through, they should ooh and ahh at its various features. All the cosmetic things, such as paint, window coverings, and flooring, should be in good shape or, at minimum, spotlessly clean.

When the house doesn't look good, it is a difficult sell. The vast majority of buyers simply won't have anything to do with it. This is true even in a sizzling hot market. When buyers are asked to pay high prices, they expect to be getting something really fine in return. A home that looks worn and torn and in disrepair doesn't fit that bill. On the other hand, if you can see beyond the home's bedraggled appearance to its true value, you'll be able to purchase it for a lower price even in a hot market.

How Much Can You Save?

Your savings can be anywhere from just a few hundred dollars to 30 percent or more off the price. It all depends on whether the property has a serious problem or just a cosmetic one—and on how the home presents itself to buyers. As noted above, the more poorly a house "shows," the less it can command, even in a tight market.

When buying a fixer-upper, it's important to use a "sharp pencil" to calculate exactly how much it will cost you to put the property back into shape. You should never pay more than the market value for any property. And the market value is a combination of the sales price plus the cost of refurbishing.

Sales Price + Cost of Fixing Up = Market Value

> Most people pay too much for a fixer-upper. They see a reduced price and think they are getting a bargain. However, unless the price is reduced to the point where they can afford to fix up the property and still not put more into it than its market value, it's not a bargain.

Where Can You Find a "Fixer"?

Fixer-uppers abound in every type of market. Most real estate agents are aware of one or two at any given time. Just ask around and you'll be shown the "dogs" of the marketplace.

Also, when checking real estate ads in the local newspaper, look for key words that will lead you to fixers. These include:

Needs TLC (tender loving care)

Handyman's delight

Scrub, paint, and save

Sweat equity housing

Earn your down payment

Always Low-Ball a "Fixer"

Even in a sizzling market, always offer less than the asking price for a fixer-upper. Remember, the easiest thing to do here is to pay too much.

Whenever I'm in the fixer market, I never pay any attention to what the sellers are asking for the property. Instead, I check out comparable properties (those in good, fixed-up shape) to establish finished market value. Then in addition to subtracting my cost of fixing, as noted above, I subtract at least another 5 percent for my trouble, and then make my offer. Sometimes my offer is tens of thousands below what the sellers are asking.

Usually my offer is rejected. But when it isn't, I know I've gotten myself a good deal.

You never know what the sellers will accept. Often the home has been sitting on the market for a long time with only other low-ball offers coming in. My offer, or your offer, may be just the one that finally breaks the sellers' resistance.

Beware of Sellers Who Do Minimal Cosmetic Work

Sellers aren't stupid. They know that in a hot market there's pressure for all kinds of homes, even fixer-uppers. So often they will take out a home equity mortgage and do minimal work, such as putting in cheap carpeting and repainting throughout.

Don't discount the effect of doing just this little bit of work. Suddenly a place that looks terrible (and that, indeed, may have all sorts of serious problems) can look pretty good. It's like taking an old, beat-up car and giving it a new coat of paint. The engine may still backfire, the transmission may be shot, and the differential may groan. But with a new coat of paint, it suddenly looks inviting.

When a seller does the minimal cosmetic work to a property, you can pretty much forget about getting it at a price that makes doing the real work worthwhile. Inevitably there will be a foolish buyer out there who takes a gander at the home, doesn't realize that only cosmetic work has been done, and offers much more than you can (if you want to get true value for your money).

This is a case of the fool in the market. The other buyer is offering too much. Don't be a bigger fool by getting into a competition and paying even more.

Power Tip 20
Look for "Out-of-Favor"
Homes

Have you ever gone to an auto dealership and noticed that there are always one or two new cars that simply don't get sold? The model may be hot, but these one or two languish on the lot. Perhaps it's an unusual color. Or maybe it's the lack (or surfeit) of features. For whatever reason, the cars seem out of favor. Yet, to get rid of them, a dealer will make you the best deal ever on just these cars.

Something similar happens with real estate. Pick any good area, such as the one in which you want to buy. Now closely examine the homes that are for sale. You'll likely find plenty with just the number of bedrooms and baths that you want. And some will have good floor plans, lot locations, landscaping, and so on. But there will usually be one or two that just don't make it. For whatever reason, they are out of favor. And while other homes sell quickly, even in a hot market, these seem to just sit there, unsold. Often their prices are substantially less those of other, more favored, homes.

If you can find one of these out-of-favor homes, it can be your bargain. Usually the sellers are willing to give some on the price, to make the sale. And if you're stretching to get into the neighborhood, this may just be your ticket to enter.

What Makes a Home Out of Favor?

Tastes change. What is considered stylish today may be considered old-fashioned, even trite and contrived, tomorrow. The same holds true for homes.

For example, today everyone in the area is looking for a ranch-style home. One plantation-style house stands out like a sore thumb. The one-story ranch homes with their rustic exteriors are getting the oohs and ahhs. This poor home with its stately two-story columns in front and its massive entry simply gets a big ho-hum.

Or maybe the out-of-favor house is a tiny bungalow built back in the 1940s, while the surrounding homes are newer and bigger. No one wants a bungalow, right? So the price is low to begin with. And the seller is willing to work a deal. Suddenly you can afford to get into the neighborhood.

Or perhaps the house has a serious problem. Perhaps it backs up to a school, an apartment building, or (probably worst of all) a strip shopping mall. This will make any property unpopular. But it will result in a lower price and more negotiating room.

> Know the difference between being out of taste and having a serious problem. A house that isn't stylish may become stylish in the future and can go up in value. A house that has a serious problem, such as being adjacent to a mall, will always have that problem, whatever the market. It will cost less when you buy, but you'll get less when you resell.

Will the Home Eventually Go Up in Value?

Unless the problem is serious, a home often will go up in value. Tastes change. Eventually the people who loved ranch homes will tire of them. The plantation style will come back in vogue. As long as there isn't a serious problem, all you have to do is live in the property and keep it up until its value catches up to its neighbors.

Keep in mind that the critical factor is not the house itself, but the neighborhood. (Remember: "Location, location, location!") You want to find the least desired home in the neighborhood and get in with the best price.

Add Value

Sometimes you can quickly turn the home around by adding value. It's not that you can change the spots of a leopard, but you may be able to change the home's style. A two-story plantation could be converted to a two-story New England. Or a new exterior could give it a Spanish look. It's positively amazing what can be done with some imagination and a relatively small amount of money and effort.

Adding landscaping can minimize many undesirable features of location, such as being near a school or mall. I once bought a home that was in a sort of hole. The neighboring lots on the sides and back looked down into it. Naturally, I got it at a good price.

The first thing I did after moving in was to plant tall fast-growing trees on the periphery. Within a few years these trees were tall. They created shade, provided a beautiful appearance, and most of all, obscured the neighboring lots. Neighbors no longer could look in. I had transformed a problem into a garden setting. The house quickly caught up to its neighbors in value, and I resold it for a healthy return.

Sometimes Whole Blocks Are in Disfavor

You may discover a bargain in a neighborhood in which one or two blocks are run down. Maybe there were several owners who let their property go. The lawns are dried up. There are weeds. In short, several homes are a mess. As a result, the entire block suffers. Home values go down, since buyers don't want to move in nearby.

On the other hand, this problem can be your opportunity. People who let their properties go often move fairly soon. (They may have let the house go because of financial troubles, and moving may be a necessity.) Once you move in, at a reduced price, you can begin taking action.

For example, you could organize the neighborhood and bring pressure to bear on less responsible owners. If there's a home owners association and it has been lax, you could help revitalize it to make owners clean up their act. You could go to the city for relief. Some cities have neighborhood beautification programs and will help you work with "bad" neighbors.

Of course, it's important to understand that there's a risk. Sloppy neighbors may continue to live in their homes for years and may refuse all attempts at cleaning up their act. There's no guarantee you can turn around a bad block. But, if worse comes to worse, the lesser amount you paid to get in will be reflected only in a lesser amount when you resell. And at least you'll be in an overall good neighborhood (with good schools and, presumably, low crime) that you couldn't otherwise afford.

Power Tip 21
Check for the FSBO Effect

FSBOs are homes that are "for sale by owner." They are always available in any market. But when the market's sizzling hot, there tend to be more of them. And that presents an opportunity for buyers who are desperate to get in.

The reason FSBOs abound in a hot market is that sellers begin to wonder just what they are paying an agent for. After all, if homes all around are selling within a month, perhaps within a few weeks or days, why pay that agent 5, 6, or even 7 percent of the selling price in commission? Why not simply put the house up for sale yourself and pocket the money?

It's easy to understand this line of reasoning. And that's why so many FSBOs crop up in a hot market.

They're Harder to Sell

What sellers are discounting, really not seeing, is that the real estate agent's services are not limited to finding a buyer. The agent performs many functions, including three that are very important.

1. *Acting as a buffer between buyers and sellers.* An agent is a negotiator, someone who can smooth the way—oil the waters, so to speak—when a deal is made.

2. *Handling the paperwork.* These days, as noted throughout this book, the deal is made not just by signing a purchase agreement. There are disclosures, inspections, loan forms, and a host of other paperwork that needs to be properly handled. This is often done by a good agent.

3. *Overseeing the transaction.* A good agent is on top of things all the time. He or she knows what is supposed to happen and in what order, and sees that it does happen so that the deal closes on time.

This is not to say that knowledgeable sellers can't do all of the above themselves. They certainly can and I've even written a book to help them do it: *The For Sale by Owner Kit,* 2nd ed., (Dearborn, 1998). It is to say, however, that many sellers don't have the expertise to pull the deal off. More important, buyers know it.

Why Buyers Don't Like FSBOs

Buyers all like bargains. But relatively few buyers are willing to jump through the hoops that a FSBO (pronounced "Fizbo") usually requires. When you're dealing directly with an owner/seller, as opposed to an agent, there are problems right from the onset.

When you tour the home, the FSBO seller tends to hover near you, wanting to show you what he or she considers the home's best features. Thus you feel constrained from walking around and seeing the place as your own.

Further, you really don't want to confide any of your inner thoughts to the FSBO seller. After all, that person is the adversary. You don't want to let the owner know that you really like the place and are willing to starve to get it.

In addition, many buyers are hesitant to tell the FSBO seller that there are things they don't like, or that there are problems with the property, for fear of hurting the owner's feelings. You might say off-hand, "That fireplace cover needs replacing." To which the FSBO seller replies, "Why? I just bought it last year. My spouse thinks it looks wonderful. What's wrong with it?"

Now where do you go? And are you willing to complain about something else? Of course, if you were touring just with an agent, you'd have no trouble saying the fireplace cover looked just like a piece of tangled metal you once saw in a scrapyard.

Finally, after the strained time you have touring the property with the owner, how do you as the buyer make an offer? With an agent, it's simple. The agent does the negotiating for you. Who does it when the other person is the seller? Are you going to trust the FSBO seller to fill out a purchase agreement for you?

What about handling the rest of the transaction, including obtaining the needed documentation? Do you or does the seller know what documents you should be given? How can you be sure everything is done correctly?

The list of problems goes on and on. Because of the difficulty of dealing with an FSBO seller, many buyers simply opt out.

Sometimes, if a FSBO seller is willing to pay half a commission, you can "hire" an agent to represent you in the transaction. The agent does all the difficult negotiation, handles the paperwork, and oversees the deal to its fruition. Of course, some short-sighted sellers determined to save money may not see things this way and may refuse to pay any commission.

Why You Can Get a Bargain

What all the above goes to show is that a FSBO is a hard sell. Even if the price is less than market, most buyers simply aren't willing to deal directly with sellers. They are afraid of getting cheated, inadvertently doing something illegal, or otherwise screwing up the deal. They feel that purchasing a house is just too complicated and too important not to do it the "right way." Besides, they can find plenty of homes that are being handled by agents.

Thus, the typical FSBO will languish on the market, even a hot market, for weeks or months until the sellers finally bite the bullet and list. Then the property sells within days.

On the other hand, you can step in, if you're willing to do the work, and buy that FSBO before the sellers give up and list it, sometimes at a good price. You can, for example, offer to buy for 3 to 6 percent less than market value. In a sizzling market, that's a savings you might not otherwise be able to find. In addition, you'll actually be getting a home, which might be difficult to come by in a tight market.

Of course, you'll have to do the work that an agent would otherwise do. That includes putting up with the sellers' ego as they tell you how wonderful the run-down place is. However, if you've bought and sold real estate before, chances are you may already know most of the drill. All that may be needed is to pay an agent to handle the unfamiliar work that's required.

Further, in some parts of the country you or the sellers may be able to hire a real estate attorney to handle all the paperwork. Frequently the cost here is less than $1,000, sometimes as little as $500.

In most residential real estate transactions the sellers will strive to make sure the deal, once struck, is carried to conclusion correctly. The sellers have to provide disclosures, allow inspections, come up with a marketable title, and so on. (Your biggest jobs are coming up with cash and financing and approving reports.) Thus, as a buyer these days, you can play the role of the innocent and make the seller do all the work. It doesn't hurt, however, to have a professional in your corner who has expert knowledge.

Power Tip 22
Take a Backup Position

Sometimes when you lose out on the purchase of a home in a sizzling market, you can back into the deal later on. This can happen if you take a backup position.

A "backup" means, essentially, that your offer either was second best or came in too late. The sellers have already accepted an offer from another party. This frequently happens in a hot market when there are multiple offers. There may be a first backup, a second backup, a third, and so on. If and when the winning buyer cannot conclude the transaction, the first backup becomes the buyer. If and when the first backup cannot complete the transaction, the second backup becomes the buyer.

Sellers are usually happy to accept backups, contingent upon the offer they've already accepted falling through. It puts the winning buyer on notice to get the deal closed, and fast.

If you're in a backup position, it means you have no rights to purchase the property unless and until the buyers before you cannot complete the purchase. Only then will you get your chance to buy.

Here's how it works. If your offer comes in late or second best, the sellers will often counter it with a backup offer at the price and terms already accepted by the winning buyer. If you accept, that may mean you will need to pay more than you originally offered.

If you happened to offer more than the winning buyer—by coming in too late with your offer—the sellers may simply counter with the contingency that if the winning deal falls through, you get to purchase. Sellers really like this arrangement because they get not only a backup buyer but a better deal. They just sit back and hope that their present buyer will not be able to complete the purchase!

Why Sellers Want a Backup Position

For sellers, having a backup offer in the wings is the best of all possible worlds. They are in a position to refuse every demand of their current buyer. No matter what the buyer wants them to do, from fixing a leaky roof to repainting the exterior, they can sit back and say,

"No!" And if the current buyer balks, the sellers know they have a secondary buyer ready to step up to the plate.

The current buyer knows that too, and consequently rarely makes strong demands. Instead, the buyer works hard to close the deal quickly. (In a situation with backups, the first buyer usually has only a very limited time—say, 30 days—to complete the deal. If it can't be completed by then, the first buyer loses out.)

Why You Would Want to Be a Backup Buyer

The backup position has certain attractions for you as well. For one thing, it costs you nothing. You can simply sit there and hope the winning buyer can't complete the purchase. For another, there's always a chance that the first deal will fall through. If it does, you are now in first position and can move forward to purchase the home you wanted.

Further, if you eventually do move forward, you're in a much better position to deal with the sellers. Usually there won't be more than one serious backup buyer. Now, if the sellers try to refuse a demand you make, they might lose the sale entirely and have to start over from ground zero. In a really hot market, that may not be much of a threat, but it should carry some weight in minor disputes.

Finally, you can be a backup buyer in a whole series of purchases. The more deals you line up, the more likely that one of them will fall through and you'll get to buy a home. Just be sure your backups give you refusal rights; see below.

How It Works

As noted, if you're in a backup position, the sellers have countered your original offer with their own, contingent upon the winning buyer's not being able to complete the transaction. If you accept their counter, then only if and when they notify you that their first buyer is out of contention will you be able to buy. At that point, if you've drawn up your purchase agreement right, you have a period of time, typically 24 to 72 hours, to agree to complete the purchase. A poor purchase agreement would commit you to moving ahead with the sale automatically (without giving you an option) if the first buyer fell through.

> Always insist on the option of moving forward with the purchase of the home if the first buyer falls through. What you want is the ability to accept or refuse the deal at that time. That allows you to make multiple backup offers. You're not committed to moving forward on any of them, unless you want to. It also allows you to reopen negotiations with the sellers if and when they notify you that their first buyer can't complete the transaction.

Other Backups

In a hotly contested purchase, there may be half a dozen backup offers. Each of the several multiple buyers is offered a position. However, except for the first backup, the others are not usually considered serious contenders. They may accept the position, but only if they are given the right of refusal. This allows them to look elsewhere.

Usually by the time things get down to a backup, at least a month has passed and the lower-level backups have purchased elsewhere, stopped looking, or simply moved away.

What You Should Beware Of

Before accepting a backup position, you should be sure that there is a strict time limit on the winning buyer's time to complete the transaction. The usual limit is 30 days. If the winning buyer has a longer time to complete the transaction—say, 60 or 90 days—there's too much chance that the buyer will work out some kind of compromise over almost any problems that arise and thus will be able to complete the deal.

As noted above, you should make certain that your backup is really a right of refusal. If not, then you will have to forgo making any other offers while the backup is in place. In effect, the sellers have tied you up, and you have to sit there waiting and hoping without being able to make any other move. It becomes a one-sided deal.

You should also be certain that the language of the agreement ties up the sellers. If their first deal falls through, then they *must* sell to you at the agreed-upon terms within the time limit you have for refusal or acceptance. In other words, they must give you the same deal that you originally agreed to.

A backup position is certainly second best. However, sometimes in a very tight market it can lead to your getting the house you want.

Power Tip 23
Consider a Cash-Only Offer

Cash is king, or so goes the maxim. It's often more true in real estate than elsewhere, mainly because financing is so much a part of home purchase transactions. That's why if you can offer cash when everyone else is offering financing, you have a better shot at making a deal.

Consider this scenario. You want to buy a property. However, the market's so tight that you know there will be at least three other offers coming in the same time as yours. So you plan on doing the usual, offering at least the asking price if not more.

Nevertheless, you're afraid that others may do the same thing. How can you make your offer stand out, be more enticing to the sellers than any others, while not offering a king's ransom?

One way is to offer a cash deal. You'll buy the home without the sellers having to worry about your qualifying for financing. As far as they are concerned, you'll pay cash. If you back this up with a short closing—say, 15 or 20 days—and a hefty deposit, you might very well beat out other buyers with financing requirements who offer thousands more than you. After all, you're offering the sellers a sure thing—a cash deal. Also, if for some reason you can't make it all happen, at the least they get to keep your deposit.

The Many Dangers of a Cash Deal

A cash offer is a great ploy, if you have cash. If you don't, it's a very dangerous strategy that can either pay off in a big way by getting you a great deal or backfire and result in your losing a substantial deposit (worse if the sellers decide to go after you for damages).

"Hold on," you may very well be saying right now. "I don't have the cash to buy a home, so who exactly are you talking to?"

Actually, I'm talking to you and you may indeed have the cash to buy, *if* you look at it from the correct perspective.

After all, aren't you getting financing to make the purchase? Most people are. And when you combine the financing you're getting with the cash down payment you're making, doesn't that mean all cash to the sellers? It certainly does.

So what a cash offer really means in many cases is that you're willing to sign a purchase agreement without the normal financing contingency that protects you in the event that you can't get a mortgage. If you fail to complete the purchase for any reason, even if the cause is that the finance company won't give you a loan, you lose your deposit or worse. You eliminate your back door. You close the loophole that gives you a way out. And in the process you give the sellers a big incentive to accept your offer.

Should You Really Take the Chance?

Cash only is a gamble that depends on two things: how much of a risk taker you are and how certain you are that you have a lender willing to supply the appropriate mortgage in a timely fashion. Be willing to take big risks and have a good lender, and you just might make it all work.

Remember, today you should be preapproved. That means that you've already gone to a lender and done all the paperwork. If you've been thorough, in addition to ordering the standard three-bureau credit report, you've supplied the lender with verifications of deposit (your money on hand) and employment (showing you have a continuing job). The lender has gone through underwriting and the loan is waiting there for you, subject only to an appraisal report on the house. Presumably, the lender can fund within days. Except for the reliability of the lender, your principal concern is the appraisal.

Some lenders, particularly those that use Freddie Mac as the underwriter, can now access appraisals electronically. A little over half the homes in the country qualify. If the one you are purchasing does, you may have already secured your appraisal electronically! E-approval will be increasingly common in the future. Ask your lender.

You've Got to Get a Good Appraisal, and Fast

What are the chances that the home will appraise for the sales price? In a hot market, it's a toss-up. Home prices are moving up so rapidly that the appraisals may lag behind. On the other hand, if you've carefully located comparable properties, you can usually feel pretty secure that the home you want to buy will appraise out.

Be aware, however, that securing a physical appraisal, particularly in a hot market, takes times. There may be lots of sales and it may simply be difficult to schedule an appraisal. For that reason, you may need to insist on a longer closing period—say, 45 days. This can negate the effects of a cash offer.

Will You Really Lose Your Deposit If You Can't Buy?

What we're talking about here is a clean purchase offer. No contingencies. You simply offer to pay cash and put up a deposit. If you can't follow through, expect to lose your deposit, or worse.

For this reason, you'll probably want to put up a small deposit. However, if you want to impress the sellers, put up a larger one. When it's a cash deal, the bigger the deposit, the more impressive the offer.

> A special caution is in order with regard to "specific performance." If you can't follow through on the deal, the sellers might not only take your deposit, but sue you for completion of the transaction (which could result in your having to pay damages). This rarely happens, particularly when there are other buyers in backup positions ready to jump in. But it is a possibility.

To reduce the risk of the sellers coming after you for more than just the deposit, you may want to insist that they (and you) sign a liquidated damages clause. This is found as an option in most modern real estate purchase offers.

A liquidated damages clause generally states that if you fail to complete the transaction, the sellers will accept your deposit as the entire amount of damages and not go after you for more. It can give you a little more protection. Be aware, however, that the liquidated damages clause may have specific conditions that must be met before the clause applies. Read the clause carefully and consult with your attorney on its effect in your state before relying upon it.

Should You Do It?

Offering to buy for cash is a desperate tactic that could well backfire. I personally won't do it—the risk is too great. But I have seen buyers successfully pull it off. If you know the risks and are willing to assume them, it could get you the house you want, even in a sizzling hot market.

See the checklist for *Strategies for a Hot Market* on pages 204–205.

3
Tactics for Successful Offers

Power Tip 24
Never Give Sellers More Than
24 Hours to Sign

Time is the essence of all real estate contracts. That doesn't mean that *more* time is better. Occasionally *less time* will more closely achieve your goals. What I'm speaking of specifically is a deadline.

If you've ever watched a telethon fund-raiser, you quickly realize that 90 percent of all the money is raised in the last hour. It doesn't matter how long the telethon is on the air, even if it's for days. It isn't until the last few moments before the telethon goes off the air that the donations really start rolling in.

In sports very often the game is decided in the last few minutes of play. Witness the two-minute drills in football just before halftime and the end of play. Or the two-minute clock in basketball. How often does everything come down to that final basket?

The same is true in getting sellers to accept your purchase offer. If you don't set a deadline for acceptance, the sellers may simply never get around to acting on it. As a result, your offer may never get accepted, even if it's an offer the sellers might otherwise have taken!

When preparing an offer, many buyers fail to consider how long they should give the sellers to accept. This is unfortunate, because time is such an important aspect of the deal. Remember, you are on the hook with the offer until the sellers reject it—or until you cancel it. With a long deadline, you're committed while the sellers aren't.

Setting a deadline forces the sellers to either accept or reject (and often counter) your offer. It puts them on the spot. It demands that they take action or risk losing you as a buyer. Further, it precludes another buyer from coming in with a better offer and undercutting yours.

The deadline is often the pressure that results in your getting the deal.

How Much Time Should You Give?

If you're willing to grant that setting a deadline is important, the remaining question becomes: How long should you give the sellers to accept? When should that deadline be set?

In my experience the shorter the time, the better. If I knew that my offer could be presented to the sellers within the hour, then I'd give them one hour to accept. This lets them know that if they want to keep me as a buyer they must act immediately. It forces them to seriously consider what I'm offering.

> Don't be afraid of having your offer rejected by the sellers. A rejection is better than no response at all. At least if the sellers reject it, you know they don't like it. If they counter, you can begin serious negotiations. If they don't counter, you can either up your price and terms or begin looking elsewhere. With a rejection, you won't be wasting your time waiting on the sellers' whims.

Of course, it's rarely the case that an offer can be presented to the sellers within the hour. One seller may be working; another may be out shopping or otherwise unavailable. They may not be available until later in the evening. When that's the case, there's nothing wrong with setting a deadline of, say, midnight of the day your offer is made. That usually gives plenty of time for presentation.

In some cases, however, it's simply very hard to get sellers together. They may be out of town. They may be on the road. There could be a dozen other reasons they can't be reached. When that's the case, I suggest you limit the acceptance time for your offer to no more than 24 hours. No exceptions!

If sellers want to be reached, no matter where they are, they can be. Today there are cell phones, fax machines, e-mail, and Federal Express. These days, being away is no excuse at all.

Don't Be Put Off by Agents Who Want More Time

Some agents are shy about putting pressure on sellers. Others aren't sure of their own negotiating skills. Still others like to linger over the fact that they at least have an offer and don't want to face possible rejection from the sellers, in which case they'd have nothing.

For these reasons and others, some agents don't like setting tight deadlines. They may suggest that it's impolite to put such a demanding deadline on your offer and that it could anger the sellers. They may say that the sellers or their broker can't be reached for at least three days. Others may suggest that because your offer is weak, it's best to give the sellers plenty of time to think it over. "Let it sit there and they'll keep thinking about it and may eventually decide to sign."

All of that is *bad* advice.

Making an offer is business and no sellers should be offended by any serious offer, regardless of the time constraints put on it. Rather, the sellers should be happy to get it!

Finally, the only reason sellers will let your offer sit without accepting or rejecting it is that they are hoping a better offer will come in. That might very well happen, if you don't eliminate the possibility by setting a deadline! You undercut the opposition by insisting on a strict deadline.

It doesn't matter whether the market's cold as an ice cube or sizzling hot. Your best strategy is always to set a serious deadline. Remember that if the sellers truly can't be contacted, you can always take back your offer and resubmit it at a later time, again with a short deadline. Or you can simply extend it.

You want to get that deal. Often the best way to accomplish your goal is to put time pressure on the sellers.

Power Tip 25
Work the Contingencies

Have you ever had a conversation in which the other party says, "Yes, but…"? The person is agreeing with you, but with certain reservations. In other words, the statement might be interpreted to mean, "Yes, I agree, contingent upon the following conditions."

A purchase agreement is like that. When you make your offer, typically you are saying you'll buy the property, subject to certain conditions being met. These conditions are called contingencies.

A purchase offer without contingencies is a rare thing. Normally, contingencies form a part of every offer. Most are there to protect you, the buyer, although some are included to protect the seller.

What Is a Contingency?

Quite simply, a contingency is a condition that must be met before the sale can be completed. It can be anything from getting clear title to having the seller's Aunt Matilda in Australia approve the documents. The sale is "contingent" upon something happening (or not happening). Another way to put it is that the sale is subject to some condition. Hence, contingencies are also sometimes referred to as "subject to's."

Probably the most common contingency in a sales agreement states that you do not have to complete the deal and are entitled to your deposit back, if you cannot get the financing you need. No loan, no deal.

You definitely want this contingency in; otherwise, if you can't get a big enough mortgage, you might lose your deposit. Making an offer without a loan contingency is a very risky thing to do. (See Power Tip 23 for why you might want to take that risk!)

What Contingencies Should You Have?

There are a host of other contingencies that benefit you. Here are some contingencies that you undoubtedly will want to have in your purchase agreement:

- You have the right to inspect the property and must approve the inspection.
- The sellers must provide you with disclosures of defects in the property and you must approve the disclosures.
- You have the right to a final "walk-through," just before the deal closes, to confirm that the sellers haven't damaged the property since you first saw it.
- You have the right to receive your deposit back if the sellers refuse to complete the deal.
- You have the right to back out of the deal if you can't get financing.

There are other contingencies that you may want to add to the offer. Suppose that you are buying the home because you're moving to the area to accept a new job. You may want a contingency stating that if you fail to get the new job, you're not committed to completing the purchase and you get your deposit back.

Or suppose you're in the process of selling your old home. You may want a contingency stating that you don't have to complete the purchase of the new home until your old one sells.

> Be sure that you clearly express your needs to the agent or attorney who prepares your purchase agreement. If there's a condition that you absolutely must have (for example, time to cash in bonds in order to get the deposit or down payment), be sure that it's in writing as a contingency. Otherwise, you may find yourself unable to make the purchase in a timely fashion and you could lose your deposit. In an extreme case, you could even be sued by the sellers for specific performance—a demand that you make the purchase (or end up paying damages).

Who Writes In the Contingencies?

A contingency must contain the proper language to be effective and legally binding. For that reason, ideally, contingencies are written in by an attorney.

However, many real estate agents are extremely experienced in this area and write in contingencies all the time in the course of doing business. (Agents may be far more experienced in the matter than some attorneys!) In practice, very often the agent will write in the contingency you want.

Whom Does the Contingency Protect?

As we've seen, the contingencies noted above protect you. They allow you to gracefully exit the deal with no bad consequences, provided something doesn't work out—you don't get your job, you fail to obtain financing, the house has unexpected problems, or your old house doesn't sell. (As we'll see shortly, sometimes inserting contingencies can actually get you a better deal.)

Other contingencies are designed to protect the sellers instead of you. For example, the sellers may insist on a contingency that says the purchase must be completed within 30 days. However, you're quite sure you won't be able to get financing, or perhaps all your cash together for the down payment, for 45 days. If you miss the deadline, you could lose the house—and your deposit!

Or the sellers may insist that you purchase the house "as is." This means that no matter what's wrong with it, they won't fix it. You may discover, after making your offer, that the roof needs replacement at a cost of $15,000. If you've agreed to buy it as is, you're out the money.

Obviously, you want to include only those contingencies that give you maximum protection and avoid those that protect the sellers. Usually the process comes down to negotiation. And therein lies the key to getting a better deal for you.

Contingencies Can Become Deal Points

A deal point is a sticking point on which the deal hinges. For example, you want the sellers to replace the broken fence around the backyard. So you put in a contingency that your purchase is subject to the fence being fixed. The sellers refuse; they say they lived with that old fence for years and they're not going to fix it up for buyers. They won't sign the deal unless you take out that contingency. Suddenly you've got a deal point. What should you do?

It depends on how important that fence is to you. If you really feel that you can't live with the deal unless the fence is fixed, and you refuse to fix it yourself, then you may simply refuse to budge. You may tell the sellers that you refuse to remove the contingency. They can then either accept your offer as written or reject it. (By the way, the negotiation process usually takes place through written counteroffers not simply word of mouth.) If the sellers accept, you've won. If they reject, you've lost your new home.

Often a better way of handling such matters is to ask yourself just how important the deal point is to you. If it's just a fence, you may calculate the cost (say it comes to $1,000) and just accept that you're going to spend a grand more to buy the home.

Or you may withdraw your contingency on the fence and make a demand elsewhere. For example, you won't insist the fence be fixed, but you will insist that the sellers throw in their double-door refrigerator, saving you more than $1,000 in buying a new one. If the sellers planned to dump that old fridge anyhow, you've suddenly compromised yourself into a deal.

Using a Contingency to Get Yourself a Better Deal

Contingency deal points can evolve over anything from the date escrow is going to close to who pays certain closing costs. There's no limit to how creative you can be with regard to contingencies. Often deals are made or lost according to the buyer's skill at negotiating contingencies.

A good way of negotiating is to find something the sellers absolutely want, and then deal over that for something else you want. For example, the sellers must have the deal closed within 25 days so they can purchase a new home. You agree, providing they fix the roof, lower the price, or otherwise accede to one of your important demands. Thus the contingency results in your getting a superior deal.

Beware of Removing Contingencies

It has often been said that the modern process of purchasing a home involves removing the buyer's contingencies one by one until none are left and the buyer is forced to close the deal. Remember, however, that contingencies really offer you a way to gracefully back out. Thus, the more contingencies you remove, the less your chance of being able to get out without a problem.

Most contingencies involve a time limit. For example, you can inspect the property and approve the inspection report, but you have only 14 days in which to do so. If you haven't removed this contingency (by approving the inspection report) within 14 days, you lose the deal. Of course, you get your deposit back, but you haven't made a purchase. Thus, in order to keep the deal on track, you effectively remove the contingency.

At the very end of the deal you may need to remove your greatest protection: the financing contingency. The sellers may limit this contingency by demanding that you get financing within 30 days. At the end of that time, either you agree to remove your financing contingency or you back out of the deal because you couldn't get a mortgage. You had better be darn sure you've got that loan locked up before you remove that financing contingency.

Don't Weigh the Deal Down With Unnecessary Contingencies

Sometimes when buyers discover the great protective value of contingencies, they insist that extra ones be placed in the purchase offer. For example, you insist that the purchase become contingent on your not losing your job before the deal closes. (You pretty much get this protection in any event, since if you lose your job, the lender probably won't give you a mortgage, and you can back out using the financing contingency.)

Or you insist that the deal be contingent on your not getting ill during the escrow period, or your spouse not falling out of love with the home, or your getting approval of the purchase from your parents. Remember, you can make the deal contingent on anything!

The problem is that each time you add a contingency, you weaken the deal. The sellers ask themselves, "Why does the buyer insist on this?" If the quickest answer is that the buyer is wishy-washy and may not go through with the deal, the sellers may simply refuse to sign. You may quash a perfectly makeable deal simply by insisting on unnecessary contingencies.

As many real estate agents have witnessed, lawyers can ruin an otherwise makeable deal by adding contingencies favoring their clients to the point where the other party simply won't go along. While legal advice is great, sometimes common sense and human nature play a stronger role.

Power Tip 26
Start With a Small Deposit

A deposit in real estate is often referred to as "earnest money." It shows that you, the buyer, are sincere in your offer to purchase—so sincere, in fact, that you're willing to put some cash at risk.

A deposit is what's supposed to entice sellers into agreeing to do business with you. There is nothing to say you can't make an offer without a deposit—you can. But most sellers won't consider it because it's far too easy for you to simply walk away from any deal that might be concluded.

> Often buyers who have weak offers will put up big deposits, hoping to impress sellers. In my experience, however, savvy sellers are rarely impressed by such tactics. They are far more concerned about the quality of the offer than the size of the deposit.

From your perspective, putting up a deposit is risky. If the sellers accept your offer and then you are unable to complete the transaction, you could lose that money. Further, while the money is tied up as a deposit, you usually aren't earning any interest on it. Thus, even though the deposit is essential to show the sellers that you really do want to purchase their property, it is money that is put at risk to you.

How Much Real Risk Is There of Losing Your Deposit?

In reality, it all comes down to how the deposit is handled in a typical real estate transaction.

Technically, any deposit you put up belongs to the sellers. After all, you are offering to buy their property; hence, they are the ones to logically receive and hold your deposit money. In theory, the agent in the transaction is supposed to turn over any deposit received to the sellers.

You are required to have on deposit enough cash to handle any check you write. However, an agent will often ask for a check even if you don't currently have enough funds in the account. The agent may say he or she won't cash the check until the sellers accept the offer, and only then do you need to make the funds available (for example, by transferring funds from a savings or brokerage account). In practice, this process seems to work fine, as long as you can come up with the money on very short notice.

In practice, however, only the most foolish agent would turn over a deposit to the sellers. The reason is simple. Suppose the deal subsequently doesn't go through, without fault on the buyer's side. In that case the buyer is entitled to a full refund of the deposit. But what if the sellers, who received that money, spent it? What if they can't come up with it or refuse to return it?

The buyer might then have to go to court to get the deposit back. And you can be sure the buyer would include the agent as a defendant in the lawsuit. The agent would then have to pay for costly litigation. It could be a real mess. For this reason, agents almost never turn deposits over to sellers.

Rather, the most common practice is to have the buyer make out the deposit check, not to the sellers, but to an escrow company. Typically the check is not cashed until a deal is signed. Then the agent immediately deposits the check into escrow, where it remains until both buyer and seller agree on its disposition.

Keep in mind that you can demand and receive back your deposit at any time before the deal is made. Until the sellers sign on the dotted line to the exact terms you have offered (or compromised to), you can withdraw your offer and redeem your deposit. (It is extremely rare for an agent to cash a deposit check before a deal is struck.) Once the deal is signed and your deposit money is sent to escrow, it is at risk.

How Do You Get Your Money out of Escrow?

If the deal moves forward and escrow closes, your deposit is normally applied toward your irdown payment. The only time problems pop up is when the deal doesn't move forward.

> There's an old rule in real estate: Make sure the purchase offer states clearly that the deposit is to be used as part of the down payment. If this wording is not included, the deposit may be handled *in addition* to the down payment, effectively raising your purchase price!

If for some reason the deal falls through, your deposit money (cash by now, since your check has gone through the system) remains in escrow. What happens to it next can be a matter of hot debate.

It's important to understand than an escrow officer is a stakeholder, an independent third party who holds all the monies as well as the title to the property. Escrow operates only on the basis of identical instructions issued by both parties. When all the instructions have been fulfilled, the escrow officer issues you a deed to the property and gives the sellers their money. This way, no one has an advantage and a fair deal is made. (Without escrow the sellers might get the money before you get title, or you might get title before they get the money—another real mess.)

The escrow instructions are based on the purchase agreement. Typically the escrow officer will read the agreement and then write up a specific set of instructions, asking both you and the sellers to sign them. Once both parties have signed, the escrow moves forward toward closing the deal.

> WARNING! Be sure to read the escrow instructions carefully. Sometimes escrow officers misinterpret contingencies or other conditions of the sale. These should be corrected before both parties sign the instructions. Otherwise, there could be a real hassle later on.

Typically the escrow instructions state that the deposit is to be applied to the down payment when the deal closes. They also state that in the event the deal is not concluded, *both* parties must sign a release before the escrow officer will return the deposit to you or give it to the sellers.

This is your control. If the deal doesn't go through, the sellers don't get the money until you release it. Similarly, you don't get the deposit back until the sellers release it to you.

Now if the deal doesn't go through, what do you think the chances are that the sellers will sign the release? True, you won't sign either, so they can't get the money. But it's your money. And it's tied up there in escrow, so you can't access it.

Typically after a few weeks, common sense prevails. If the sellers really aren't entitled to the money because you backed out of the deal on the basis of some contingency, they will sign. The advantage to them is that this closes the would-be deal and allows them to move on with the sale of the property.

For your part, if you're really not entitled to the money, you may want to sign for the same reasons. On the other hand, if you refuse to sign a release, the only recourse the sellers may have is to take you to court to get the money out.

Why You Should Put Up a Smaller Deposit

The point to keep in mind here is that your deposit is always at some risk. One way to reduce that risk is to put up a smaller deposit.

But, it can be argued, won't the sellers be less impressed by less money?

Yes, that's probably true. On a house with a selling price of $400,000, a $10,000 deposit is probably the minimum that would impress sellers. On the other hand, except in a hot market with competing offers, a $1,000 deposit might work just as well. After all, the sellers are presumably interested in selling their property, not claiming a deposit. If you're a solid buyer (as witnessed by your preapproved loan) and you offer a reasonable deal, the size of the deposit probably won't be a large factor in the decision to accept your offer.

I have sold many properties with buyers offering just $1,000 as a deposit. And I've bought many the same way.

You Can Increase the Deposit Later

Remember that in today's world, a deal is not really a deal until all the contingencies—principally the disclosures and inspection—have been removed. Therefore, savvy sellers realize that you're almost certainly entitled to your deposit back right up until the time you sign off on those contingencies.

Therefore, sellers will often accept a small deposit, but then insert a clause asking for a larger deposit once the contingencies are removed. This is a reasonable and fair way to handle the problem.

After all, by the time you're ready to remove the contingencies, you're presumably convinced that you want to buy the property and are satisfied with the deal. Since you have to come up with the money for the down payment within a few weeks anyhow, why not increase the deposit (which, remember, goes into the down payment)?

How Small a Deposit Should You Put Up?

Technically, as noted earlier, you really don't need any deposit (although a deal without a deposit is in reality no deal at all). However, $1,000 is normally enough to seal the deal on any property. This is particularly the case when you agree to up the amount as soon as you remove the principal contingencies.

However, in a sizzling hot market with competing offers, this tactic won't work. Suppose there are two similar offers, one with $1,000 as deposit and the other with $10,000. All else being equal, which one do you think the sellers will take? Which one would you take?

Offering a small deposit in a normal to cold market works just fine. In a hot market, it's a poor tactic to use.

Power Tip 27
Always Demand Inspections
and Disclosures

Would you buy an automobile without driving it, or at least looking it over or taking it to your mechanic to check out? Would you buy a used car without asking the seller if there was anything wrong with it? If you would, then you're more trusting than I am.

Most people these days want and feel entitled to know what they are getting. Instead of the maxim "Caveat emptor" (let the buyer beware), the current rule is "Let the buyer know." This is particularly the case in real estate.

Why Do You Need an Inspection?

An inspection is just what it says it is—an opportunity to have an expert look closely at the property you are considering purchasing and getting both an oral and a written opinion as to its condition. You need an inspection to know just what it is you are buying and to know whether you are getting your money's worth.

For example, you may be purchasing a 35-year-old home for $200,000. After looking over recent sales, you determine that this home is indeed worth the money. You make an offer and it is subsequently accepted.

Now you hire an inspector to go through the home. She determines that the concrete slab (forming the floor) is badly cracked, the roof needs replacement, the plumbing is leaking, the electrical wiring is not up to code, and there are a host of other problems. You get estimates from contractors and find it will cost $50,000 for repairs.

Do you still think the home is worth $200,000? If not, your inspection contingency lets you back out of the deal (or renegotiate, as we'll see in the next Power Tip).

Always go along with the inspector during the inspection. The oral comments often are far more revealing and detailed than what you will find in the written report. The reason is that inspectors frequently try to cover themselves against legal problems by couching written language in disclaimers, caveats, and banalities. They are much more candid when you're there in person. Besides, when you go along you can ask questions and have them answered.

Why Do You Need Disclosures?

Disclosures, now required in most states upon the sale of a home, tell you what the seller knows about the condition of the property. If, for example, the house is tilted to one side, the sellers should disclose that fact to you.

You need the disclosures for at least two reasons. The first is so that you will know what you are getting. For example, if the disclosures say that there are some leaks in the roof, you can now hire a roofing contractor to determine if the roof can be patched or must be replaced and how much that will cost. Depending on the results, your disclosure contingency lets you back out of the deal or negotiate for the repair with the sellers.

The second reason for disclosure is to put the sellers on record as to what they know is wrong with the property. If they say there's nothing wrong and your inspection doesn't turn up anything, you'll undoubtedly presume that everything is okay. But if after moving in you discover that the sellers filled and painted over big cracks in the foundation in order to conceal them, your chances of hauling them into court to pay for repairs are excellent. After all, they're on record as saying there were no problems and here you discover that they concealed big troubles. You've been victimized and the disclosures provide written evidence of that fact. (The sellers can't later say, "We told you about it and you ignored it!")

How Do You Get an Inspection?

You have to demand an inspection when you present your offer. It must be written in as a contingency; either you get the right to inspect the property and approve the report or your don't buy. Many modern real estate contracts automatically provide an inspection contingency.

You'll have to pay for the inspection and find an inspector. Inspectors are listed in the yellow pages of your phone book. Be aware, however, that home inspection is not yet regulated in most parts of the country, meaning that anyone can be an inspector, qualified or not. As a result, you have to carefully check out the person you hire.

I suggest looking for an inspector who belongs to a local trade organization as well as one of the two national trade organizations, ASHI (American Society of Home Inspectors) or NAHI (National Association of Home Inspectors).

> Look for someone who is likely to know about construction such as a structural engineer or, even better (if you can find one), a retired city or county building inspector who is now making extra money by handling home inspections for buyers.

How Do You Get Disclosures?

Disclosures may be required by law. For example, in California the seller must provide the buyer with a set of disclosures listing defects in the property. You, the buyer, then have three days to approve or disapprove of the disclosures. If you disapprove, you are not required to complete the transaction and your deposit is returned. Disclosures are handled in other ways by other states.

In the event there is no statutory procedure for handling disclosures, you can demand them from the seller by inserting a disclosure contingency into the purchase agreement. The contingency should insist that the seller provide full disclosure of all defects and that, if you disapprove the disclosure statement, you have the right to back out of the deal. A good real estate agent or attorney will be able to insert the proper language.

Only a fool would buy a pig in a poke, and here we're talking about an item that is probably worth hundreds of thousands of dollars. Don't jeopardize your investment. Get a home inspection and disclosures and make your purchase contingent on approving them.

Don't confuse a "final walk-though" with a home inspection. The former occurs just before the deal is set to close and is designed to allow you to be sure the sellers haven't changed or damaged the property since you first saw it. That's quite different from a thorough home inspection, which is designed to uncover any structural or other problems with the property.

Power Tip 28
Never Stop Negotiating

Many of us subscribe to the Old West credo that a deal is finished when both parties shake hands on it. If that's your way of thinking, then be prepared to get skinned alive when you buy real estate. The modern credo is "Never stop negotiating"—even after the deal is signed, even after escrow has opened, even after escrow has closed and title has passed to you. If you truly want to look out for your own interests, you won't stop negotiating, ever!

Yes, this is a bit of an exaggeration. Nevertheless, those who do get the best deals in real estate are often those who keep right on negotiating as long as, so to speak, there's anything left on the table.

Negotiate as Part of Making an Offer

The entire process of making an offer involves negotiation. You purchase a home at a certain price for specified terms, including contingencies that allow you to back out in certain circumstances. The sellers read your offer and then either accept or, more likely, counter at a different price and with different terms, perhaps eliminating some of your contingencies and modifying others by limiting them, for example, in terms of time. Thus the sellers may agree that you can have an inspection, but you must approve the report within, say, 14 days.

Back and forth it goes with counteroffers, and counters to the counteroffers and counters to the counter to the counteroffers. This is the negotiation process and, depending on how good you are at it, you'll get a better or worse deal.

If you get a deal that's acceptable to you and is the best you feel you can get, and if the same is true for the sellers, there's agreement and everyone signs. The presumption is that the deal is made.

Don't count on it.

Negotiate Over the Disclosures

A wise buyer knows that the really tough negotiations frequently don't start until after the deal is signed. Usually the next negotiation takes place over the disclosures. Within a few days of signing, you should receive a list of defects in the property as revealed by the sellers. (If you get the list *before* negotiations start, then this point is moot.)

If your offer was properly filled out (or if your state gives you rights here), you now can back out of the deal without penalty. If something seriously wrong is revealed, you may want to simply say no, take back your deposit, and move on.

Or you may want to negotiate some more.

You do this by letting the sellers know (through their agent, if they have one) that you disapprove of the disclosures because of the problem(s) they reveal. However, you're willing to go through with the deal if the sellers either repair the problem or reduce the price. If it's price you want, you indicate what you consider to be a fair price (sometimes a figure significantly lower than what was originally agreed upon), and negotiations begin again.

Typically the sellers will balk. But if they want to sell and there is a problem, they very likely will counter your offer. Back and forth it goes until both parties feel they can live with the same set of terms. If something significant was revealed in the disclosures (or if you said that, in your view, what was revealed was important), you may get a significant price reduction or better terms.

Negotiate Over the Home Inspection

The next negotiation frequently occurs over the results of the home inspection.

It's rare that a home inspection, even of a brand new home, will reveal nothing amiss. Usually there's something, even if it's just leaking faucets. Depending on the severity of the problem(s) discovered, savvy buyers now open negotiations all over again.

How can you do this? Remember, a good inspection clause is actually a contingency that, in effect, makes the purchase subject to the buyer's approving the inspection report. You don't approve. There's no deal—unless the sellers are willing to come down in price or up in terms.

Keep in mind that problems such as these usually arise two weeks or so after the deal was originally signed. During those two weeks the sellers have begun making plans to move. They may even have put down a deposit and made a deal on another home. They are counting on your deal going through.

Now, suddenly, there's a hitch. As the buyer, you are balking at something that came up in the inspection. You can bet that the sellers are going to be eager to smooth over the problem, if they can. I've seen deals where the price was knocked down $3,500 to handle a problem with paint, $17,000 for a problem with a roof, and $35,000 to accommodate a problem with the structure.

Why would the sellers be so accommodating? It's not that they want to. It's just that once a problem is revealed, it will have to be dealt with one way or another, either with you or with other buyers. It might as well be you, since you're already involved in the deal.

Further, sellers sometimes simply get desperate to sell. Although they were adamantly against lowering their price or giving you a better deal during the initial negotiations, now they simply lay down and roll over. I've seen it happen.

> You may negotiate a cash settlement without actually having a disclosure problem corrected, provided the lender doesn't object. For example, the sellers may lower the price $5,000 over a leaking roof. However, instead of replacing the roof, you have it patched for $500 and pocket the difference (at least until the next rainstorm).

Negotiate During Escrow

Some buyers with a lot of what might be called gall negotiate right through escrow. As the sellers get more and more used to the idea of their home being sold, the buyers keep coming up with new concerns that can be resolved only by further concessions from the sellers.

I've heard buyers say that they drove by and became aware that the window trim was damaged. They then wanted several hundred dollars off the price to have it fixed. If not, they would simply hold off on buying the home. Yes, these buyers stand a chance of losing their deposit (and more), but the sellers won't get it either without going to court. In the meantime, the sellers' house is tied up. It simply becomes easier for the sellers to acquiesce than to fight.

In a very slow market, buyers may demand a reduction in price because of market conditions. They simply tell the sellers that prices are going down. The house is no longer worth what it was when the offer was accepted. Either the sellers accommodate with a lower price or the buyers refuse the deal.

Once again, the sellers have options, none of them particularly good in a down market. And many will acquiesce to placate an irritable buyer.

The sellers could refuse a buyer's new terms, then demand the deposit, or even demand specific performance (the buyer either goes through with the purchase or, more likely, pays damages). But few sellers really want to go to court and fewer actually do. Buyers with gall and the willingness to risk a lot have pulled off some amazing deals in this fashion.

Negotiate After You Own the Property

It is possible to get a better deal even after the escrow has closed and you take possession of the property. This frequently happens when buyers find something amiss, and demand that sellers make it good.

In one case, the buyers discovered after they moved in that the sellers had allowed their pets to run wild over much of the home. A urine smell permeated the wall-to-wall carpeting in several rooms. The smell had not been detected earlier because the windows were always open when the buyers inspected the property. Further, the sellers had failed to disclose this problem.

It's important to understand that animal urine in carpeting cannot really be removed. The smell will remain, often permeating the padding and even the flooring beneath.

The buyers demanded that the sellers replace not just the carpeting in the rooms with the problem, but the carpeting throughout the house, since it was all of a kind. They said it wouldn't look right to have just a few rooms fixed. After conferring with their agent, the sellers agreed.

Then the buyers picked out the carpeting, which was valued at close to $15,000, installed. The sellers balked, but when confronted with the cost and possible outcome if the matter went to litigation, they sent the buyers a check for that amount.

As long as there are problems, you can negotiate with the sellers. In some cases, even if the problem is something you imagine, you can still negotiate and win concessions simply because the sellers don't want to bother with the nuisance.

Remember, to paraphase Yogi Berra, the deal isn't over until it's over.

> Don't pressure sellers too far. If you insist on unreasonable demands, they may simply refuse and buckle down, ready to fight you legally. That could mean you'd lose the house and have legal problems to boot.

Power Tip 29
Find Sellers Who Are Highly Motivated

Why would a kid sell his favorite baseball glove? Why would a woman pawn her wedding bands? Why would a home owner offer to sell for less than his house is worth?

There's only one answer to all three questions—strong motivation. Perhaps the kid wants to buy baseball cards, and selling the glove is his only way of raising money. Maybe the woman is getting divorced and wants to get rid of the reminders of her failed marriage. Perhaps the home owner wants to get out because of a desperate financial situation.

Whatever the motivation, there's always an answer. And if you can provide that answer, you can not only help the motivated person get what he or she wants but also get yourself a good deal.

The key, of course, is discovering the motivation of the seller. Often sellers will conceal their true motive for fear that buyers will use it as leverage against them. However, in so doing they limit their ability to get what they most want, a timely sale.

> People who are highly motivated often have to decide what they want most—more money or a quick sale.

How Do You Learn What Motivates Sellers?

I've found that the best way to uncover sellers' motivation is simply to ask. I try to make it a point to tour property at a time when sellers are likely to be home, in the evening around dinner or on the weekends.

Isn't this an inconvenience to the sellers? Probably. But as anyone who has ever sold a property quickly learns, if home owners want to sell, they must make their property available when buyers want to look. And that's frequently at times inconvenient to the sellers, as in the evening and on weekends. It's just part of what goes with selling.

While I'm looking at the house, I also talk with the sellers. I ask them: "Do you like this house? Is the neighborhood good? Are there any problems I should know about?"

Most sellers will quickly begin defending their property, pointing out how much they've enjoyed living there. Unless there's some serious problem, they will usually emphasize that nothing is wrong at all.

Then I simply ask: "Why are you moving?" It's a simple question and requires a simple, but convincing answer. The sellers know it and they know I know it. So most often they will tell the truth.

Perhaps they are moving because of a job change to a new location. If they have to be at the new job by next week, they are highly motivated. If it's within three months, they aren't.

Or perhaps they are moving because of a divorce. The property has to be sold immediately so the money can be divided up. Again, the sellers are highly motivated, but there could be difficulty in getting estranged partners to sign off on the deal.

Or the sellers are having financial problems and the house is in foreclosure. If they can't find a buyer soon, they could lose everything. Very highly motivated.

Of course, not all sellers are candid. Some will be evasive. I personally think this is a mistake on their part. Being highly motivated means that you want to or must sell quickly. Keeping that fact a secret doesn't help you get a buyer, particularly in an average to cold market. Letting everyone know you are highly motivated, on the other hand, will draw in lots of buyers.

I also ask sellers' agents about their clients' motivation. Surprisingly, agents are often very candid. Technically, an agent should not reveal whether a client is highly motivated unless directed to do so by the seller, since it will undoubtedly affect my offer. But in practice, things tend to slip out. Perhaps the agent tells all in the hope of helping the seller by securing offers.

A "highly motivated" seller is one who is under strong pressure to sell quickly. This type of seller is most likely to accept a lower price as well as lesser terms.

If both these routes prove impassable, my next step is to consult with the neighbors. There's nothing to prevent me from meeting people in the area and introducing myself as a prospective buyer.

In these matters, I admit to being a snoop. I always walk the neighborhood around any home I'm considering buying. I try to do this on a Saturday morning or on an early evening when the neighbors are out and about. I introduce myself, explain that I'm considering buying the home down the street, and casually ask if it's a nice neighborhood. Then, as part of the conversation, I often bluntly say, "If it's such a nice area, I wonder why they're selling."

Most neighbors will bend over backward to tell you the good and the bad. And that frequently includes the true motivation of the sellers, if they know. One nosy neighbor can provide all you need to know about the sellers' motivation.

What Do You Do With the Knowledge?

As indicated in the last Power Tip, motivation means there is a problem somewhere. Solve the sellers' problem, and you can often get a better deal for yourself. For example, if the sellers are highly motivated because they need to move quickly, give them a fast sale—and a lower price (see the next Power Tip).

Most highly motivated sellers need cash, fast. If you can make an offer, even a low one, that gives them cash in a short time—say, a 20-day escrow—you've sweetened the pot and they are more likely to accept it. You may be able to do this if you have your ducks all in a row—if you're preapproved for financing and have your cash down payment in hand.

Are You Taking Advantage?

Don't feel that you are taking advantage here. In fact, you are probably providing a way out for the sellers from a difficult problem.

Remember, you don't create the sellers' motivation; you simply respond to it. It's a win-win situation. As a buyer, you naturally want a property at the lowest possible price. Maybe keeping the price low is the only way you have of getting into a neighborhood you desperately want to live in. Perhaps you have limited funds and you're offering your maximum. Or maybe you just want to make a profit.

Regardless, you have your own motivation in buying. If you can make a deal that satisfies your motivation as well as that of the sellers, everyone wins. After all, it's a free market. If there's a better offer than yours, the sellers will take it. If there's no better offer, then the sellers may be thrilled to get yours.

Power Tip 30
Sweeten a Low Price Offer
With Better Terms

I once saw a sign in a printing shop that said,

> Price.
> Quality.
> Time.
> You take two, I'll take one.

The meaning was clear. If you wanted a rush job, you would have to pay more, or accept lower quality. On the other hand, if you were willing to wait, the price could be low with high quality. And so on.

Most things in life are trade-offs. Making real estate offers is no exception. If you offer the sellers a good price, you can usually demand more favorable terms. On the other hand, if you low-ball the sellers, then you'll probably have to trade that off for terms more favorable to them.

These rules hold for a normal market. In a very hot market, just to get the property away from competing offers, you may have to come up with a better price at less favorable terms. And in a very cold market, where sellers are desperate to get rid of their properties, they will both lower their price and offer more favorable terms.

Keep in mind that in a sizzling hot market, the price/terms trade-off won't work. You will probably have to offer the best price and terms you can, just to get the house.

How Do You Know What to Trade Off?

What terms do the sellers want so badly that they'd be willing to lower their price to get them?

Some are obvious. If you're giving the sellers a second mortgage, you can increase the interest rate. However, most modern transactions are cash deals, so chances are you won't have that opportunity. On the other hand, some sellers want to move quickly or to delay their move. If you're accommodating, they might consider your low offer more seriously.

In the last Power Tip we went into sellers' motivation. Now's your chance to use what you learned.

Tailor Your Offer

Be creative. Suppose the sellers are retiring and want to downsize. Do you offer them the typical cash-to-loan deal?

Probably not. When they sell and downsize, chances are they are going to end up with a fistful of cash. They are probably planning on banking that money and may be intending to live off the interest. Of course, bank interest may be dismally low, around 4 to 6 percent.

So why not offer them a second mortgage (or even a first, if the property's paid off) at a higher interest rate? The money would be secure, with the property serving as collateral. And the interest rate would be significantly higher than what they would get at the bank. In exchange, on your side you could demand a lower price or even less cash down.

Will the sellers take it? You won't know until you try. They just might!

On the other hand, perhaps the sellers are divorcing and need a quick cash sale. Why not offer them cash to a new loan and a 20-day escrow? You can check with the lender that preapproved your financing (see Power Tip 1) to see if it can be done. Today, depending on how active the market is, it's possible.

The sellers can be out quickly with the money they get from your offer—provided, of course, they are willing to accept a lower price.

Or perhaps the sellers are moving to another area. They need to sell in order to buy their next home. But, they also need a place to live for 90 days until their new house is finished.

So you offer to rent back the home to them for just enough to cover your payments. They get both to sell and to stay until their new home is finished. You get your lower price.

Be careful with rent-backs, in which the former owners become tenants. You're now a landlord with all the problems that go along with ownership, including potential eviction if your tenants don't pay their rent and refuse to move out.

Your options are limited only by your imagination. Find out what the sellers want and give it to them in exchange for a lower price (or a lower down payment).

Give In on Price for Better Terms

The reverse approach also works. Sometimes sellers have heard that homes like theirs are selling for X dollars. In order not to get "cheated," they refuse to sell for less than that amount, no matter how good the terms you present.

Okay, live with it. Instead of trying to get a lower price, meet the seller's price. Then demand terms that are more favorable to you.

For example, give the sellers their price. In exchange, demand that they give you a second mortgage at below-market rates. If the going rates for a second mortgage are 9 percent, insist on 5 and perhaps compromise on 6 percent. Since you're going to need a mortgage anyhow, this will give you one that saves you money each month. (Any lender can calculate your exact savings. Try Internet lenders such as www.eloan.com or www.mortgage.com. Their on-line calculators can quickly give you the answers.) Money is money. You trade off the higher price you pay for the monthly savings on interest.

You may need other concessions. For example, you may want to close escrow on a specific day. You pay the sellers' price and they give you that day. Or you may want them to put in a landscaped backyard. They agree, provided you pay the price.

Again, the list is endless.

What You Need to Get Started

As noted earlier, you need to know the motivation of the sellers. If you can offer them a better deal, they may become flexible on price or even down payment. (Down payment is often a function of how big a mortgage the lender will offer, and the sellers may have very little to do with that.)

You also need to define where you stand. Can you be flexible? Must you have only a lower price? Or can you stand paying a higher price in a trade-off for better terms to you? If you can be flexible, sometimes you can create an incredibly sweet deal that includes paying a high price!

Always keep in mind, however, that your ability to negotiate depends in large part on the market. The hotter the market, the less room you have for negotiation. The colder the market, the more you can get away with.

See the checklist for *Tactics for Successful Offers* on pages 205–206.

4

Profiting in a Normal or Cold Market

Power Tip 31
Look for More Expensive
Homes Than You Qualify For

As we've seen, the first order of business when house hunting is to get preapproved for financing. Besides giving you a tool to leverage a seller, the process also lets you know how big a monthly payment you can afford, the biggest loan you can get, and, coupled with your down payment, the most expensive house you can afford.

The second order of business is to ignore what you've just discovered and look for more expensive homes.

It's not that the lenders are wrong. It's not that you'll be able to purchase a more expensive house. It's that by the time you get through making an offer and negotiating with the sellers, chances are that the price will come down to what you can afford.

How much more expensive a house should you look for? In all but a sizzling market (where homes are sold at or even above asking price), look for homes that are 5 to 7 percent more than you can afford. In a cold market or one in which prices are actually declining, look for homes that are 10 to 25 percent more than you can afford. (See the next Power Tip for a further explanation.)

The Advantage of Stretching

There are two reasons to stretch to get the most expensive home you can afford. The first is personal satisfaction.

There's a correlation between home price and quality. Usually the more the home costs, the better it is. More expensive homes are bigger and better located, have larger lots, offer more amenities, are in better condition, and so forth.

The more you can afford, therefore, the better a home you'll get, almost always. Pay more, stretch to pay the most you can afford, and chances are you'll be happier with the property you get.

The first home I bought after marrying, I purchased because it was a good deal, even though it was at a much lower price than I could afford. However, it was in a neighborhood that I really didn't care to live in and was smaller than we needed. I regretted the purchase the entire two years we lived there—and never made that mistake again.

The second reason to stretch is that you will usually make more money on the home by spending more for it. It's not always true, as we'll see shortly, but it's usually true. Here's why.

In a normal to hot market where prices are advancing, you can expect that the home you purchase today will be worth more tomorrow. If you factor in inflation, the home could be worth far more. During the era between 1950 and 1990, homes appreciated at an annual rate of about 5 percent in most parts of the country.

Of course, that doesn't mean they went up 5 percent every year. Some years they didn't go up at all. Other years they accelerated to 7 or even 8 percent.

Further, some areas of the country didn't experience such rapid appreciation during that period. Maine and other parts of New England, for example, saw decades of stagnant prices. On the other hand, other parts of the country, particularly the West Coast, saw a higher annual price appreciation.

Thus, most of the time just buying a home means you'll make money on it. However, the bigger the home, the more money you'll make (in terms of absolute dollars). It only stands to reason that if the house costs more and prices go up, you'll make more. (Five percent appreciation on a $200,000 home is $10,000; on a $400,000 home it's $20,000. The percentage of appreciation is the same, but the absolute increase in money is more.)

It's the same argument that says you'll make more money if you buy 200 shares of a stock that goes up instead of just 100 shares. You'll make twice as much.

On the other hand, you will invest more, at least when buying stocks (assuming you don't buy on margin). Which brings us to the second rule of stretching: Put as little of your own money into the house as possible (while still being able to afford the payments).

If you put 20 percent down, the typical down payment, you have a leverage factor of 4 to 1. For every $1 you invest, a lender has invested $4. But if you put 10 percent down, you increase that to a leverage factor of 9 to 1. For every $1 you invest, the lender has invested $9. When the house appreciates and it comes time to sell, the higher your leverage factor, the more profit you make.

For example, the house costs $100,000, you put $20,000 down, and the house appreciates 5 percent to $105,000. You've just made 25 percent on your money. ($5,000 is 25 percent of your $20,000 investment.) On the other hand, if you put only $10,000 down on the same house and it appreciates $5,000, you've made 50 percent on your money. ($5,000 is 50 percent of your $10,000 investment.)

Investors have known of this leveraging phenomenon for years. At least while prices are appreciating, they will buy the biggest house with the smallest down payment they can afford, thus leveraging themselves into ever greater profits.

Be Wary of Getting Overextended

The big problem with this strategy, unfortunately, is that if the situation changes (you lose your job, you get sick and can't work, or the economy turns downward), you could be in big trouble. If you're at your maximum and something happens, you might not be able to make the payments and you could be forced to sell earlier than you anticipated, for a loss. In a worst-case scenario, you might not be able to sell at all, and could lose the home to foreclosure.

An owner with a big equity can often ride out a dip in the housing market cycle. On the other hand, an owner who bought with a very small down payment often is forced out. This is one reason that lenders prefer mortgage borrowers to put down as much as possible.

A decade or so ago few Americans worried about the downside risk of investing in real estate. (Even if they bought a home as their personal residence, it was still an investment.) The thought pervading the country was that real estate prices only went up; they never went down. (A similar feeling pervaded the stock market at the end of the century.)

Of course, recent downturns give the lie to this assumption. Markets move up, and they move down. If you're overextended, you can make big bucks on the upward movement. But you stand to lose in a big way on the downturn.

All of which is to say that to make more money in real estate, buy a bigger house with a smaller down payment. Do the reverse to reduce your risk. And go for more than you think you can afford, because after you negotiate the price down, it will probably be within your range.

Power Tip 32
Low-Ball Your First Offer

Except in a sizzling hot market, don't expect to pay the asking price. Sellers typically ask more than they are willing to take for a home. Sometimes the sellers will come down 5 percent. In a cold market, they might come down 10 or even 20 percent or more.

Sellers usually assume that there's going to be some dickering over the price and that they will have to come down some. Thus, in a normal market, you can expect to get a home for anywhere from 3 to 7 percent less than its asking price. As a result, if you look only for homes whose asking price is at your maximum, you will find that you end up with less house than you can afford—and probably desire.

How Much Less Should You Offer?

I have been asked "How much to offer?" countless times, usually by reporters who want a simple answer they can write up in their columns. They want to hear, "Offer 5 percent less." Or 10 percent less. Or whatever.

Indeed, if you must have a rule of thumb, then here it is. Except in hot markets,offer 5 percent less. Just keep in mind, however, that your offer is probably going to be way off—far too high or too low.

The real answer to how much you should offer requires a bit of investigation on your part. Then again, if you're planning on spending the big bucks to buy a home, it's probably worth a half hour's time learning how much to offer.

What you need to do is to huddle with a real estate agent and get two different statistics, both of which any agent worth his or her salt will have. The first is the median sales price in your area. What are houses selling for? (Remember, the median is the middle—as many houses are selling for more than this number as less.)

The next number you need is the median asking price for homes. How much are homes listing for in your area? The two numbers will always be different.

Now it's simply a matter of determining the percentage difference between the two numbers. That's the median amount that most sellers are reducing their price in order to get a sale.

Finding the Median Price Reduction

$$\frac{\text{Median Sales Price}}{\text{Median Asking Price}} = \text{Median Price Reduction}$$

$$\frac{\$150,000}{\$160,000} = 9.375\%$$

All else being equal, you can expect to purchase your home for the asking price less the median price reduction. In our example, that reduction happens to be a whopping 9.4 plus percent.

Some real estate boards don't make you hunt for this information. They provide it. They simply give you the difference between asking price and sales price for homes listed over the past month, three months, or six months.

Don't Blind-Offer the Median Price Reduction

Every situation is different. Some sellers are more motivated to sell than others. If you discover this, you will probably want to offer even less than the median.

Similarly, if the house has a problem, needs fixing up, has a major detracting feature (such as being on a corner lot or backing up to a shopping center), you may want to offer less. However, the price may have already been adjusted down to compensate for the problem.

On the other hand, the house you like may be fixed up. The sellers have put a lot of money into it, and expect to get a lot out. Don't expect to get the usual price reduction here.

Use the median price reduction as a guide. Then offer more or less depending on the house, the sellers, and your actual situation.

Always Low-Ball in a Slow Market

Of course, if the market is falling, it's a whole different ball game. In a cold market, where there are far more homes for sale than buyers and houses are sitting unsold for six months to a year or longer, you're definitely in the driver's seat. You can make all sorts of ridiculous offers and have sellers, at the least, seriously consider them. Indeed, making very low offers in a cold market should be your absolute rule. But be wary of making offers that aren't really low enough.

In a really bad market, such as occurred at the beginning of the 1990s, almost no offer was too low, and many offers that came in and were accepted were actually too high. Consider a house selling for $200,000. You offer an amazing 20 percent less, or $160,000—and the seller accepts! You've gotten yourself a great deal, right?

Maybe, and then again, maybe not. What if the market continues to fall and a year later your home is worth only $140,000? Now what kind of a deal did you get? During the last real estate slump, price declines of 30 percent or more in many markets were not unusual. Often buyers who purchased before the bottom, though they paid far less than the asking price, still did not get a good deal.

The problem, of course, is that it's just as difficult to determine the correct price in a falling market as it is in a rising one. Market price is determined by past sales. But when the market is slipping, past sales are not a true indication of current value. Today's value may be less. And tomorrow's value may be far less.

That is one reason that so few people actually buy in a falling market. They fear getting in before the bottom and losing money.

However, if you want or need to buy, keep in mind that during the last housing slump, which was the most severe since the Great Depression of the 1930s, housing prices fell by an average of about 32 percent. In areas less affected by the overall downturn, the slump was limited to only about 20 percent. In other areas, where there was severe unemployment and economic distress, prices fell by 40 percent or more.

The best advice is that when the market is falling, wait before you buy. If you can't wait, try to fathom the depths of the downturn in your area, and then use historical prices as your guide. I know that's not a clear-cut path you can easily follow, but it is better than simply jumping in and blindly offering 5 percent less than the sellers are asking.

Power Tip 33
Look for REOs and
Foreclosures

People are always losing their properties to foreclosure. Sometimes it's because of a job loss. Other times it's a divorce. I've even seen cases where the owners simply grew old, didn't have relatives or friends to help them, didn't keep up the payments, and lost their property.

Foreclosures are most plentiful when the market is bad. At that time, people who get in trouble and can't make their payments also often can't find buyers to get them out from under their problem. As a result, when they don't (or can't) make their payments, the lender is forced to take the property back.

On the other hand, when the market is normal, there are fewer foreclosures. And when it's hot, foreclosures almost cease to exist.

Foreclosures can present a buying opportunity for you, if you're careful. They can offer you a way into a neighborhood at a price you might not otherwise be able to afford. On the other hand, there are many pitfalls to avoid.

What's the Big Benefit of a Foreclosure?

Let's say it's an average market, not hot or cold, and you want to buy in a particular neighborhood. Only the least expensive home is $325,000 and the maximum you can buy, based on your loan preapproval and cash in hand, is $275,000. You're $50,000 short of getting into the neighborhood you want.

However, you discover that a home in the area is in foreclosure. It's dilapidated and vacant. The owner isn't around. A sign posted on it from a lender warns vagrants and vandals away, noting that the property is in the final steps of foreclosure.

So you go down to the assessor's office (or wherever tax records of properties are kept in your area) and find out who owns that property and the owner's last mailing address. (Some title insurance companies can also look this up for you.) If that doesn't work, you check with the neighbors or even look up the owner's name in the local phone book.

In any event, you discover that the owner is now residing in a motel on the other side of town. You meet with that owner, who has given up on saving the property. You learn that the owner will lose the property in three weeks. You give the owner a nominal amount of money to sign a quit claim deed over to you, and then you go out and secure financing to pay off the existing loan and lender. All of a sudden the property is yours.

If you've done it right and there aren't unexpected complications (which there usually are), you have bought the property below market, perhaps far enough below to get the house you want in the neighborhood of your dreams.

Is it that simple? No, far from it.

What Are the Hazards?

There are many pitfalls. Here's a list of just a few.

- You may not be able to get financing in time to pay off the existing lender before foreclosure. In that case, the lender will take over the property and you'll have no claim to it.

- There may be other liens on the property—a second, third, or fourth mortgage, for example—that have precedence over your quit claim deed. By the time you discover these and pay them off, you may find that you've paid more for the property than it's worth! Or there could be tax claims or judgments against the owner. Unknown liens are probably the biggest single problem in dealing with raw foreclosures.

- It could cost a small fortune to bring the property back into a state of repair. One of the most common errors that would-be foreclosure buyers make is underestimating the cost of refurbishing a run-down property.

- After you've done it all and have secured the property, the original owner could come back with a claim that you used undue influence in getting him or her to sign away the property. You could find yourself embroiled in messy litigation, from which you might not emerge the victor.

How Do You Avoid the Problems and Still Get the Property?

You can be diligent and careful. You can check the title to the property for hidden mortgages and liens. You can get the owner to sign a comprehensive sales agreement. You can get estimates for repairs prior to leaping into the deal.

Or you can wait until the property has gone through the entire foreclosure process and then attempt to buy it from the lender. This is called the REO market.

What Are REOs?

REO stands for "real estate owned." It is the one department in a lending institution that you are least likely to hear about. It usually has no offices open to the public. It isn't likely to be part of the lender's phone listing. Even if you do somehow get in touch, you may not find anyone there who wants to talk with you.

The reason is that foreclosed property causes an accounting switch in the lending institution, a switch that can have wide-ranging and deleterious effects. Essentially, when there's a producing loan on a property, it is considered an asset. When the lender is forced to foreclose and take the property back, it switches from the asset side and becomes a liability. Too many REOs and the lender could go out of business, closed by a regulatory agency. REOs tend to lower a lender's stock value. As a result, lenders don't like to broadcast the fact that they have REOs. (Some lenders will even shy away from admitting that fact to consumers!)

Nevertheless, lenders must get rid of these properties, in effect converting them to cash, which can then be profitably loaned out again as a mortgage (an asset). To accomplish this, they often list the property with agents. Hence, one proven method of finding REOs is to contact real estate brokers.

However, many lenders don't want REOs listed on the multiple listing service, since it broadcasts their existence; instead they will have only one or two brokers in town handle the properties. Thus, it behooves you to find out which agents in your area specialize in REOs. (Asking around among different lenders or even agents at several real estate companies will usually get you the information.)

When the market is really bad, the big lenders in the area often have so many REOs that they form their own real estate company to handle them. Also, major secondary lenders such as Fannie Mae and Freddie Mac, as well as mortgage insurers such as the FHA and guarantors such as the VA, sometimes run their own REO programs. These are often advertised in the Sunday section of local papers.

What's Better: Raw Foreclosures or REOs?

The big advantage of REOs over foreclosures is that they usually offer you clear title. When the lender takes the property back, it clears all the "clouds" on the title, liens, and other defects affecting it. Thus, when you get the property, you can be fairly assured that it's clean. You would, however, be wise to secure title insurance at that time, just to be sure.

Further, in order to get a better price for REOs, most lenders will also clean up the property. This usually takes the form of cosmetic fixes such as painting, reglazing, replastering, or whatever else is necessary.

Sometimes you can negotiate with a lender over the repair work, particularly if the lender is offering to carry back a new mortgage for you. (Some lenders will, others won't, carry back mortgages.) You might agree to purchase if the lender will kick back a certain amount of the price as you complete repair work. I recently was involved in a $400,000 property in which the lender forked over $35,000 for repairs—nearly 10 percent of the purchase price.

On the other hand, because the property and title are in better shape, the lender may demand more money than you would have paid if you purchased the REO during the foreclosure process. Thus, REOs tend to be more expensive. (This is also the case because the lender may have put lots of money into the property—the original mortgage payoff amount plus lost interest plus all the costs of foreclosure, which can be heavy.)

Thus, you have a trade-off. Buying a property raw in foreclosure will often get you a much better price deal. But the risks are much higher. Buying a property as a REO will get you a much cleaner deal and, sometimes, better financing. But the price will be higher.

Learn the Field

If you're serious about looking for foreclosures, spend some time investigating the field. Get acquainted with someone who has handled foreclosures in your area (such as a real estate agent, an attorney, or a loan broker). The procedure is far easier once you've seen it done by someone else.

Also, learn thoroughly the foreclosure procedure in your state. It varies significantly across the country. In the West, trust deeds are used as mortgage instruments. The lender can often foreclose on these within a few months and without going to court. On the other hand, many parts of the country still use judicial mortgages. These can be foreclosed only by going to court, and typically the procedure takes far longer.

Each method has different cutoff dates that determine what stage the foreclosure procedure has reached and whether or not it's wise for you to jump in. Learn the procedure well for your area. Also, check into my book *How to Find Hidden Real Estate Bargains,* rev. ed. (McGraw-Hill, 1991).

Power Tip 34
Look for Auctions

When the market's cold, and sometimes even when it's not, sellers will try to drum up interest in their properties by holding an auction. The theory is that the auction itself will draw in buyers, and the competitive bidding will result in higher prices.

Sometimes it works for sellers. But sometimes it works for buyers. If you're looking to buy a house and auctions are being held in your area, it's usually worth your time to at least check them out.

An auction can be held by an individual owner, by a lender that has several houses, or by an auction company that represents several lenders. The advantage and the perils are similar in all cases.

What Are the Pros and Cons?

The big plus of buying at auction is getting a bargain. You might purchase a home for far less than its market value. The big negative is that you might end up paying too much. You could end up buying a house for more than you would have paid simply by going through the usual process of submitting an offer.

> Some of the best auctions I've been to (from a seller's perspective) have been held outdoors in a big tent with refreshments offered free to those attending. Usually a big crowd shows up and as the professional auctioneer works it, people lose their normal restraints and begin competing against each other for homes. This drives the prices far too high, from a buyer's perspective.

What Should You Look Out For?

There are a number of perils when buying by auction. Here are several.

1. *The sellers hold a reserve.* A reserve, even though it may not be announced, is a minimum price below which the sellers will not let the property go. For example, even though the bidding may start at $50,000, the sellers may reserve the right not to sell below $100,000.

Recent legislation in many states now requires that sellers disclose if there's a reserve.

2. *There could be problems with the title.* Usually if an auction house or lender handles the sale, the risks are minimal. But with an individual seller, you never know. The way to avoid this problem is to make sure any offer you make is contingent on the seller delivering clear title and title insurance to you.

3. *You might end up with unfavorable financing.* In a regular transaction, you'll go out and get your financing beforehand. With an auction, sometimes the seller has prearranged some sort of financing and you may be obligated to take it. Further, you may be required to put up a heftier down payment (20 percent minimum) than you would otherwise. You could, of course, go out and get your own financing, and some auctions encourage you to do so. But often there's a very narrow window of opportunity to get the loan. And if you don't perform in time, the next highest bidder moves into place.

4. *You might not have a good opportunity to examine the property.* In a regular transaction you should be given disclosures by the sellers as well as a fairly long opportunity (typically two weeks) to inspect the property. In an auction, you may be presented with disclosures and a completed inspection report at the time of the auction and be asked to sign off immediately. (Some states allow this. Other states give you a few days to examine disclosures before being required to sign off.) Too often, buyers rush into auctions on homes that they haven't truly examined, sometimes seeing the property for the first time only on the day of the sale. Fearful that if they took enough time to truly consider the property, someone else might buy it out from under them, they rush into making bids at auction.

5. *You may simply be unfamiliar with the auction process.* How many movies have you seen in which a bystander at an auction sneezes or waves at someone, and suddenly buys the lot being auctioned? It's not quite that simple to make a bid. A certain knowledge of what you're doing is required. It includes knowing how much cash you must put on deposit, when it must be put up, how long before you must come up with the down payment if you win, what the bidding procedures are, and so on. When the sale is conducted by an auction house, these procedures are usually clearly spelled

out. When the seller is an individual, they may not be so clear. Be sure you understand the ground rules before you bid.

Is an Auction a Good Way to Buy a Home?

Auctions can be bargains, particularly if there are few or disinterested bidders and the seller is desperate to get out. However, in my experience, a buyer can usually get a better deal by making low-ball offers on other properties.

Power Tip 35
Work With Upside-Down
Sellers

When sellers are upside down, it doesn't mean they are standing on their head, although it may feel like that to them. Rather, it means that they owe more on their property than it is worth. When you're right side up, you have positive equity in your property. When you're upside down, you have negative equity.

Sellers get to be upside down in a variety of ways. The most common is when they buy high at the peak of the market, and then try to sell later on when the market has fallen. If they put little cash down, the value of the home may have fallen below the amount of their mortgage, and they're upside down.

Another relatively recent phenomenon that has led sellers into this predicament is obtaining 125 percent financing. The sellers borrowed 25 percent more than their home was worth. They assumed that, over time, the price would go up and everything would work out.

However, perhaps prices didn't go up. Or maybe the owners had to sell sooner than they anticipated. In any event, the market failed to catch up with their mortgage and now they owe more than their home is worth.

Where's the Advantage?

Upside-down sellers are in a tight fix. They aren't going to get any money out of the sale. However, they are usually desperate to preserve their good credit, so they can get another mortgage and buy a home in the future. Thus, they are willing to work with a buyer on any solution short of foreclosure.

You, on the other hand, are looking for a good deal—presumably a home below market price. If you can help the sellers out with their good credit, and get the home at a good price, it's a terrific deal for all. Remember, you'll have relatively little competition in trying to make this deal. Few buyers want to work with sellers who owe more than the market value of their home.

Sometimes upside-down sellers can have the lender transfer the mortgage onto a new home they are buying, thus getting out from under. However, this presumes they are buying another house, that it is for enough money to justify even the current mortgage amount, and that the lender is willing to go along. Most lenders aren't that reasonable.

Get the Lender to Accept
a Short Sale

The key to helping the sellers and buying the property at a good price is to get the lender to accept a short sale. This means that the lender agrees to write off a portion of the mortgage. If the mortgage amount is $125,000, the lender agrees to accept, for example, $100,000 as payment in full.

Why would a lender do this? The reason is that under the current market conditions, the loan may not be worth more than $100,000. Thus, if the lender takes back the property, it will have an asset it can't sell for the full loan amount. Further, in any foreclosure, it will have high costs.

In 1998 the average cost of foreclosing to lenders was in excess of $20,000. This included costs of foreclosure, back interest, penalties, back taxes, and the cost of maintaining and later refurbishing the home.

Finally, the lender must believe that the sellers will let the property go to foreclosure if they can't get a sale. If the lender believes the sellers will keep on making the payments no matter what, it will never agree to a short sale.

Your role in all this is that of the white knight. You're agreeing to buy the property, albeit at a low price. You're willing to end the agony for everyone, clean the slate, make the problem go away.

In order for lenders to agree to a short sale, they must be approached with a deal in hand. The sellers frequently don't have the heart for all the details. That is your role as white knight.

> When sellers are upside down, sometimes it's the costs of sale, including the commission, that put them there. If they sold FSBO, they might be able to get out from under without a short sale. In many cases there's no agent involved, simply because there's no money to pay the commission.

The procedure is simple. You have the sellers contact the lender to find out who to talk to about working something out. Usually only the sellers can lead the way. Then you (and the sellers) go down and present your legitimate offer—the way out.

Usually the lender will want to think on it. That means it has to go before a committee, which will seek to discover if there's any other way out. If your offer turns out to be the best financial choice (more money than going through foreclosure), the lender may accept it. You've got yourself a deal. The sellers have gotten out from under.

Do Lenders Often Agree to a Short Sale?

The success of short sales usually depends on the market. If conditions are poor with few sales and declining prices, lenders are much more likely to accept than if the market is more normal, with occasional sales. You can forget about getting lenders to accept a short sale in a hot market. They would rather take the property back. They may feel they can resell it themselves and make a profit!

Are There Any Dangers?

As long as everything is handled above board with title insurance to protect you, and the lender and sellers sign off, the deal shouldn't be a problem for you. There could, however, be a problem for the sellers.

In order to convince the lender that they are willing to let the property go, the sellers may have to withhold mortgage payments for a few months. If the lender reports this to a credit bureau, it may adversely affect the sellers' credit. In addition, many lenders report short sales to credit bureaus. However, this is a small price to pay compared with how adversely the lender's credit would be affected by a foreclosure.

In addition, the Internal Revenue Service frequently construes a short sale as a forgiveness of debt. (The lender forgave a certain portion of the mortgage owed.) Debt forgiven is considered income. Hence, the sellers could end up paying taxes on the "income" they received when the lender agreed to a short sale!

See the checklist for *Profiting in a Normal or Cold Market* on pages 206–207.

5

Get Lenders to Work for You

Power Tip 36
Get the Right Type
of Mortgage*

Mortgages come in all sizes and shapes. Some may be well suited to your needs. Others may do more harm than good. What you want is a loan that fits you like a glove.

Your first consideration is usually the interest rate. How low can you get it? That depends on your creditworthiness.

In the past, in order to get almost any kind of mortgage you had to have good credit, a strong income, and a past history of repaying what you borrowed. Today, it's a different story. Almost anyone can get a mortgage regardless of qualifications. However, those with the best qualifications get the lowest interest rate while those with the worst qualifications pay more. Today, there's a mortgage available for virtually everyone—just not at the same interest rate or with the same down payment.

Are You a Prime Borrower?

Prime borrowers get the best mortgages, meaning the lowest interest rate. How do you know if you can get a prime mortgage? A lender will tell you.

When you get preapproved or otherwise apply for a mortgage, you'll be asked to fill out a questionnaire containing about 60 items. It will cover a broad range of questions about your financial condition as well as your borrowing history. After you complete the questionnaire, the lending officer (usually a mortgage broker) will secure a credit report, and from the information thus gathered you'll be given a score.

Several organizations handle the scoring process. The largest is FICO (Fair Isaac). This private agency takes a look at your credit history and comes up with a three-digit score. Typically if you score close to 700, you'll qualify for a prime mortgage at the best rate. If your score is below, you'll have to get a lesser mortgage at a higher rate.

---

*Portions of the material for this Power Tip were taken from Robert Irwin, *Buying Your Home on the Internet* (McGraw-Hill, 1999).

It's important to understand that scoring is arbitrary and little things can mean a lot. For example, if you apply for credit more than three times in a six-month period, it could lower your score. If you have more than three new credit cards, it could lower your score. On the other hand, if you have loads of money in the bank in reserve, it could raise your score. If you put more money down (say, 30 percent), it could raise your score astronomically. Many people are simply amazed at the score they get, for good or bad.

What Does Being a Prime Borrower Mean?

Prime borrowers can get a "conforming" loan. A conforming loan has the lowest interest rate and often can require the lowest down payment. (There are conforming loans available for 5 percent down—or even less.) A conforming loan will pass the underwriting standards of the two big secondary lenders, Fannie Mae and Freddie Mac. There are maximum limits on conforming loans, currently $240,000.

The company that actually lends you the money will most likely subsequently "sell" your mortgage to one of the big secondary lenders to get its money back so that it can lend the funds again. Of importance to you is that with a conforming loan you'll be getting a mortgage at the lowest possible interest rate.

Most mortgage brokers and other lenders that offer mortgages are actually offering conforming loans. If it turns out that you're not a prime borrower, they may not be able to help you get a mortgage, but may instead refer you to other lenders.

What Does Being a Subprime Borrower Mean?

If your score means you're less than prime, a position called subprime, you can still get a mortgage. You'll just have to pay more. It really depends on how far off prime you are. Lenders use a rating scale from A through D. A rating of B (meaning a few credit problems) still gets a pretty good loan. A D gets a loan at high interest rates and a low ratio of loan to value.

If you are subprime, chances are you won't get a conforming loan. However, many institutional lenders such as banks and mortgage bankers have programs for subprime borrowers. There are also many credit companies that specialize in the subprime borrower. Today, getting a mortgage is a matter of how much you're willing and able to pay. If you are a subprime borrower, it can just mean that you have to put up a bigger down payment, or accept a higher interest rate and monthly payment.

What If No One Will Lend to You?

Even if you have terrible credit, you can still get financing of one sort or another. You may be able to "assume" or take over an existing mortgage. Some older FHA (Federal Housing Administration) and VA (Veterans Administration) mortgages require no qualifying.

You may be able to get equity financing, in which the lender really doesn't care a whit about you, but only about the property. You may be able to get seller financing. Here the seller carries the "paper" or mortgage. Many sellers are willing to do this if the market is soft and they're having a hard time selling.

We'll discuss these types of mortgages in the next few Power Tips.

What Types of Mortgages Are Available?

These days there are more mortgage types available than you can shake a stick at. We've touched on a couple above. Let's look at a few more with brief explanations, so you can decide which is most suitable for you.

Should You Get a Fixed Rate Mortgage?

The traditional fixed rate mortgage has helped finance residential real estate for the past 70 years. The interest rate is fixed at the time you get the mortgage and does not vary over its term. If it starts out at 7 percent for 30 years, that's what it remains over the entire 360 payments.

The advantage of the fixed rate mortgage is that you always know what your payment is going to be. Since the interest rate is fixed, so is the payment. Further, if interest rates in the market rise, you're not going to be affected. Your rate will remain the same.

The disadvantage is that the interest rate for a fixed rate mortgage tends to be higher than the initial interest rate for an adjustable rate mortgage (ARM). However, in a stable or even a falling market, the differential typically is low. A fixed rate is usually disadvantageous only when the market rate is high.

In general, the time to go for a fixed rate loan is when interest rates are low. You lock in the low rate. When interest rates are high, an ARM may be a better alternative, particularly if it gives you an option to switch (without additional cost) to a fixed rate at a later time. (Some ARMs offer a switch window at year 3 or 5 of the mortgage.)

Should You Get an ARM?

In an adjustable rate mortgage the interest rate and payment fluctuate over the term of the loan. Because it often carries a lower initial interest rate, an ARM is most frequently used when interest rates are high and the borrower needs a lower rate to qualify for a mortgage. It's also useful when the borrower plans to keep the mortgage for only a short time (and will then resell the property) and wants a lower interest rate during that period.

To induce borrowers to go with an ARM, lenders may offer a "teaser." When borrowers ask how much the ARM's interest rate is, they are usually told the teaser rate, which may be as much as three points less than the current market rate. For example, the teaser rate may be 5 percent, while the market rate for fixed mortgages is 8 percent. This is usually quite an inducement to borrowers who otherwise would go for a fixed interest rate.

> Keep in mind that the teaser rate is only for a short time. After that, the ARM goes up to market rate (or higher).

Index and Margin. To determine the actual interest rate you will pay on an ARM, there are two factors to consider: the underlying index and the margin. The index reflects the cost of borrowing money in a particular market—for example, the one-year T-bills rate, the average cost of funds to lenders, or some other well-known and easily accessible rate.

The lender then adds a specific margin to the index—say, 3 percent. Thus, if the index happens to be 5 percent on a given day and the margin is 3 percent, your interest rate is a combination of the two, or 8 percent. Note that while the index fluctuates, the margin does not.

The Adjustment Period. Another critical feature to look at in an ARM is the adjustment period. How frequently can the lender adjust the mortgage rate up or down?

The adjustment period for a given loan is arbitrary, and each lender will specify its terms in the loan documents. However, different lenders, and even the same lender, will offer different loans with different adjustment periods. Therefore, borrowers need to pick and choose. Some of the more common adjustment periods are monthly, every six months, and once a year.

It's usually to your advantage to get the longest adjustment period possible. This gives you the greatest stability. On the other hand, lenders want the shortest adjustment period. This gives them the greatest protection against interest rate hikes.

One of the biggest problems with ARMs is their uncertainty. You never really know what the interest rate, and hence your periodic payment, is going to be tomorrow. It's this uncertainty that causes many borrowers to forgo ARMs.

Caps. Borrowers fear increases in mortgage payments caused by unlimited interest rate hikes on ARMs. To help reduce borrowers' fears, lenders frequently put "caps," or limits, on the ARM. They limit either the amount the interest rate can rise (or fall) or the amount the monthly payment can rise, or both.

Although most borrowers agree that interest rate caps are beneficial, the limits can be deceptive. Caps don't really give as much protection as they seem to. The reason is that they are set so high. Often for caps to kick in, interest rates have to reach historical highs, and that's unlikely. Caps are more protection for the long-shot than for month-to-month payments.

Some ARMs also set a maximum limit (payment cap) on the amount that the monthly payment can be raised each adjustment period regardless of what happens to the interest rate. This has an unusual and profound effect on the mortgage. Sometimes interest, which is charged against the mortgage, cannot be paid because the monthly payment is not high enough to accommodate it—it is capped. Therefore, the excess interest is added to the mortgage principal.

It's called "negative amortization," or interest on interest. Most government mortgages allow up to 25 percent of the original mortgage amount to be added interest. In other words, you can end up owing 125 percent of what you borrowed because of negative amortization.

Does your mortgage have negative amortization? It is something that is often hidden from view, unless you know what to look for in the documents. Although the negative amortization terms are usually explained in those mortgages in which it occurs, many people simply don't understand the implications. It means, quite simply, that if interest rates rise rapidly, the amount you owe may rise as well. You could end up owing far more than you originally borrowed!

Steps. Many ARMs set a maximum limit on the amount that the interest can be raised each adjustment period. Regardless of where the real interest rate has moved, the interest rate on the mortgage can be adjusted upward (or downward) only at predetermined amounts or steps—say, 1 or 2 percent. Let's say your adjustment period is every six months, and during the latest six-month period interest rates have jumped 3 percent. If your step is 1 percent, your interest rate cannot go up more than 1 percent during the current adjustment period. (However, it could rise an additional 1 percent the next period and the next, so it eventually reaches the market rate.)

Nearly all ARMs have steps that limit the hikes in the interest rate per each adjustment period. These limits are typically anywhere from 0.5 percent to 2.5 percent per adjustment period. Thus, regardless of what index the mortgage is tied to, the interest rate cannot be hiked more than the step amount each period.

Keep in mind that the smaller the steps, the greater the lag time when there is a sudden jump in interest rates. (Of course, a sudden decline would not be felt as quickly either.) Most people want a mortgage with small steps.

Should You Get a Balloon Mortgage?

"Balloon" in real estate finance means nothing more than a single mortgage payment (usually the last) that is larger than all the others. For example, you might get a second mortgage for $10,000 that is all due and payable in three years. During the three-year period, you might pay interest only. If the interest is 6 percent, you pay $50 a month. However, at the end of the three years, you still owe the full $10,000. (Remember, you were paying interest only.) That last payment, for the full principal, is the balloon.

Any mortgage can incorporate a balloon. We'll discuss several of the more popular ones in Power Tip 40.

Be wary of mortgages with balloons. When they come due, you need to have the money to pay them off. That may mean you will either have to sell the property or refinance. It's usually a good idea to insist on a clause in a balloon mortgage that provides for automatic refinancing (even if it's at a higher interest rate) at the balloon, just in case.

Should You Get a Biweekly Mortgage?

In a biweekly mortgage, the borrower makes a payment every other week instead of the traditional monthly payment. Since there are 52 weeks in the year, a payment every other week results in 26 "half payments" or 13 full payments. With a biweekly mortgage, therefore, each year you make the equivalent of 13 monthly payments instead of 12.

Biweekly mortgages are set up so that the extra payment each year goes to principal. Thus, over the life of the loan an amazing amount of interest is saved. As a result the mortgage can be paid off years early. In almost a painless way, you can cut almost a third off the time it takes to pay off a 30-year mortgage.

The biweekly mortgage allows many people to painlessly and effortlessly increase their principal payments. However, keep in mind that a biweekly mortgage is not for everyone. It works best when you are salaried, getting paid on a weekly or biweekly basis. You can easily budget your money to take care of the payment that way and probably won't feel the extra expense very much. On the other hand, if you're paid monthly or work for yourself, the biweekly setup can be a disaster. You won't have the money handy on a biweekly schedule.

The time to establish a biweekly mortgage is when you first get financing. Look for a lender that will set the program up for you. (Not all lenders will.)

If you already have a mortgage or find a lender that won't do this for you, you can set up a biweekly program yourself. First, however, be sure your mortgage contains no prepayment penalty (described in Power Tip 39).

It couldn't be easier. Every two weeks simply deposit half the mortgage payment into a checking account. Then once a month pay your mortgage payment from this account. (You can set up the system electronically with some banks so the deposit will automatically come from your paycheck and the payments will automatically go to the lender.)

At the end of a year, you should have the equivalent of an extra month's payment in the account. Now, simply send this to the lender, specifying that it must go to principal, not interest. (If you don't specify the purposes, the lender very likely will just consider it the next monthly payment.) You've added the equivalent of a monthly payment to your principal and have made a significant step toward paying down your mortgage.

Of course, there are companies that will do this for you for a fee. However, why pay someone else to do what you can easily do for yourself?

Should You Go for an Electronic Mortgage?

If you are a prime borrower you may be able to get a mortgage, including funding, within 3 days. This is incredibly fast, since the typical mortgage takes 20 to 45 days to secure.

Fast mortgages are basically conforming loans. They are under-written electronically through Freddie Mac and Fannie Mae. They are handled primarily by computer.

Many mortgage brokers, including some that are on-line, can handle these types of mortgages. The procedure is essentially the same as for any mortgage. After you fill out an application, a credit report is secured and you are scored. If you meet the profile requirements, the underwriter indicates that you will be approved. It's then a matter of getting a mortgage lender to move quickly.

When asking about an electronic mortgage, whether in person or on-line, ask specifically for "automated mortgage underwriting." If the lender doesn't know what you're talking about, go to a different source.

What About Government-Insured or Guaranteed Loans?

The VA (Veterans Administration) has a guaranteed loan program and the FHA (Federal Housing Administration) offers an insured program. Usually these agencies don't actually loan money. Instead they either guarantee or insure a mortgage that you obtain through the lender (in the event you default on the payments).

Qualifications are stringent. The VA requires you to be a veteran of military service during certain time periods. (Check with the VA for the current periods.) For the FHA, you must qualify almost as rigorously as an applicant for a conforming loan—that is, you must be a prime borrower.

The advantage of these mortgages is the low down payment, or in the case of a VA loan, no down payment. The disadvantage, at least in the past, has been the low mortgage amount, although the loan amounts allowed are rising.

In the past these loans have been assumable—that is, transferable to a new borrower—with a catch. Unless the person who assumed the VA loan was also a veteran, you remained liable for repayment, even if the new borrower didn't make the payments! Recently, FHA loans have become more difficult to assume, with the new borrower required to qualify as if applying for a new loan.

In addition, with lower down payments required for some conventional loans, the advantages of government mortgages have diminished.

Should You Consider a Home Equity Mortgage?

There's really not much difference between a home equity loan and a second mortgage. The term "home equity" is a marketing slogan that banks and other lenders have devised to induce property owners to borrow money on their homes.

Home equity loans can be used for virtually any purpose, from providing a college education for the kids to fixing up the property. Usually the lenders don't care. (Specific fix-up loans available through the FHA must be used to improve or remodel property.)

The interest on home equity loans can usually be deducted, up to certain limits (often a $100,000 loan maximum). There are other conditions as well, so check with a good accountant before assuming that your home equity mortgage interest is fully tax-deductible.

Some home equity loans are actually revolving lines of credit, much like credit cards. The loan is set up for a specific amount of money—say, $100,000. Then you borrow against it and pay only interest monthly. At any time you can pay down the principal without penalty. Usually there is a maximum lending period of 10 years, after which you can no longer borrow but must instead pay back the existing balance over a 20-year period.

The interest rate on home equity loans is typically a couple of points higher than on conforming first mortgages.

For quick credit, you can't beat home equity loans. Once set up, they're in place whenever you need them. Instead of having to borrow cash at very high interest rates (often 20 percent or more) on credit cards, you can borrow it on the home equity loan, typically for half that amount.

Keep in mind, however, that in order to get this type of financing, you must have considerable equity in your property. Generally speaking, your combined mortgages (first plus home equity) cannot exceed 80 percent of the property value.

Should You Get a Jumbo Mortgage?

What if you live in a high-priced area such as metropolitan New York or Southern California? What if the average home in your area costs over $300,000 or, some cases, over $500,000? How do you get financing?

The answer is a "jumbo" loan. If you need a mortgage above the conforming limitation, you operate under a different set of rules.

Most mortgage brokers, savings banks, or other lenders offer jumbos. The procedure for getting one is essentially the same as for a regular mortgage: Fill out an application, provide the required documentation, get an appraisal, and if everything checks out, get approval.

What's different is who offers the mortgage. With conforming loans, the lender funds the mortgage, then resells it to a secondary lender (Fannie Mae or Freddie Mac). With a jumbo, generally speaking the lender keeps the mortgage in its own portfolio. That's why jumbos are often called "portfolio loans."

Jumbos are readily available in those areas of the country where they are needed. However, they tend to cost about half a percentage point higher in interest. And you must still be a prime borrower to qualify for one.

A hybrid version of the jumbo is the "piggyback." Here you get two loans, the first a conforming loan up to the maximum amount allowed, then a second mortgage that goes the rest of the way up to the money limit you need. The interest rate on these loans is a blend of the conforming rate and the higher jumbo rate, which usually means a combined slightly lower interest rate and payment for you than a straight jumbo. Of course, you make only one monthly payment, with the lender separating out the amount that goes to the conforming loan and the portion that goes to the jumbo.

A jumbo can be either a fixed rate mortgage or an ARM. It can have a balloon feature. The big difference with a jumbo is the amount borrowed.

Power Tip 37
Don't Pay a Fee to a
Mortgage Broker

The most popular method of securing a mortgage these days is to use a mortgage broker (MB). Unfortunately, along with their popularity has come a small minority of MBs that take advantage of borrowers. Your goal in using an MB is to get service, not get taken advantage of.

An MB is a company (or sometimes an individual) that retails mortgages. Perhaps the easiest way to understand the MB's function is to compare it with the old days (less than 10 years ago!). Back then, when you wanted a mortgage you checked around with banks or savings and loan institutions (S&Ls). Sometimes you had to check with a dozen or more to get a sense of what the market really offered and where the best rates and terms were.

In order to service you, the borrower, these banks and S&Ls had to operate expensive "storefronts," mortgage lending centers. In those days every branch office had a lending officer.

Then came mortgage brokers. Many of these companies were created by former lending officers of banks and S&Ls. They opened up storefronts (or Internet Web sites) and offered to handle the retailing of mortgages for the lenders. The MB would deal with you, the consumer; the lender would stay in the background.

Thus, banks, S&Ls, some insurance companies, and other mortgage lenders began "wholesaling" their product. They offered them to the MBs, in effect, at a discount. The MBs, in turn, "retailed" the mortgages to consumers.

A Mortgage Broker Versus a
Mortgage Banker

A word of explanation about the difference between mortgage brokers and bankers and the preapproval letters they can issue. *Mortgage bankers* are banks that make real estate loans. However, unlike commercial banks, which you will find on many street corners and in many supermarkets, they do not offer the usual services of a bank, such as checking or savings accounts or uncollateralized loans. They offer only mortgages and sometimes not directly to the public. They are, however, legitimate lenders.

Mortgage brokers, on the other hand, are salespeople whose product is a mortgage. They often work for as many as a dozen or more lenders (such as banks, mortgage bankers, and even some insurance companies). They are, so to speak, the front office for the lender. They solicit borrowers (such as yourself) and try to fit you to the lender that offers the mortgage most suited to your needs. They broker mortgages. For this service they are paid a fee, from the lender. They do not normally have any money of their own to lend.

What Is the Mortgage Broker's Fee?

The difference between the wholesale and retail price is what the MB gets. It's typically around 1 to 1.5 percent of the *mortgage* and averages between $1,500 and $2,000.

> It's important to understand that the lender pays the mortgage broker's fee, not you. While it does come out of the mortgage you obtain, it is not an extra fee that is tacked on.

Thus, when you deal with an MB, you are normally dealing with what amounts to the storefront operation of the lender. Your rate and costs in dealing with the MB should be no different from dealing directly with the lender. Lenders normally won't undercut their MBs by giving you a better deal if you go direct.

What's the Advantage of Dealing With a Mortgage Broker?

The big advantage to you is service. Most MBs don't deal with just one lender. Instead, they represent many lenders, sometimes dozens, sometimes as many as 70 or 80. Thus, when you go to a mortgage broker, the representative can line you up with a lender that is offering the mortgage best suited to your needs. (There are literally thousands of mortgage products out there, each slightly different from the others.)

Further, instead of having to shop around for the best rate and terms, you can one-stop shop at the MBs. By representing many lenders, a good MB can immediately let you know which one is currently offering the best rate and terms.

What's the Problem With Mortgage Brokers?

Unfortunately, as the market for MBs has grown, so have a few unscrupulous MBs who seek to take advantage of borrowers. This is particularly the case when the market is strong, rates are low, and many people want to finance a purchase or refinance an existing mortgage.

Some MBs have taken to demanding a separate fee from you, the borrower. This is often described as additional points on the mortgage.

A point represents 1 percent of a mortgage. One point on a $150,000 mortgage is $1,500. Half a point on a $100,000 mortgage is $500.

Here the MB is getting paid twice. You are paying on the front end, while the lender is paying on the back end. Don't stand for it.

There are plenty of MBs around who are willing to accept the single payment from the lender. If you find an MB who wants double payment, walk out and go elsewhere.

How Do You Identify the Extra Fee?

When a few MBs first started charging borrowers an additional fee, they simply tacked it onto the RESPA (Real Estate Settlement Procedures Act) fair estimate of costs they were required to give mortgage applicants. Since most borrowers weren't aware of the charge, they didn't recognize it and simply assumed that it was a standard fee.

However, more recently, as savvy borrowers have been alerted to this problem, some MBs have found that they can't get away with listing their charge out front. Their customers simply won't stand for it.

So, instead, they have asked lenders to add the charge in as part of the loan costs. Some lenders have gone along with this. Thus, the lender may charge you an additional point or two and list it as a "loan brokerage" fee or some similar term. In other words, it's a fee paid to the lender that is then, in effect, kicked back to the MB. It's in addition to the fee that the lender normally pays to the MB.

Is this legal? Maybe not. But that doesn't mean it isn't happening.

To avoid the extra fee, you must pay scrupulous attention to the RESPA fair estimate statement and question any fee, particularly a large one, that seems unusual. It may be listed as a "loan origination" charge (some loan origination charges are legitimate, as in the case of FHA loans). Lenders and MBs have become creative in their terminology. It may be a "one-time add-on fee" or simply, "additional points." Or whatever.

Your best method of knowing for sure that you're being overcharged is to fall back on the old method of checking around. Call several MBs to find out what their charges are. Even better, check out some of the mortgage Web sites on the Internet. They usually post their fees up front. You can then quickly determine what the going rates should be.

On the Internet look for:

www.eloan.com

www.mortgage.com

Power Tip 38
Lock In the Loan

Lock-ins aren't important when interest rates are falling. They are vital, however, when rates are going up.

A lock-in simply means that the lender agrees to hold to a certain interest rate (and number of points) for a set period of time, typically between 30 and 45 days, no matter what the money market does.

For example, mortgage interest rates are rising. (Rates rise and fall in cycles over time.) At the time you apply for your mortgage, the rates are 7 percent. However, it's going to take a while for you to close your deal, probably around a month. During that time, interest rates could rise, perhaps significantly.

If rates rise to 8 percent, your monthly payments will go higher. In a worst-case scenario, you might no longer qualify for the mortgage you need and you could lose your deal.

> The monthly payments for a 30-year, $200,000 mortgage at 7 percent are $1,330.68. However, at 8 percent the payments jump to $1,547.48. That's an increase of $217 a month. While you might qualify for the mortgage with the lower payments, you might not qualify with the higher ones.

Ask for a Lock-In

When rates are rising, ask to have your loan locked in. This means that the lender guarantees the interest rate (and points), provided you can close your deal within a set period of time. You are assured of keeping the monthly payment you were originally quoted.

Be aware, however, that in a rising market that time restriction is critical. If you have 30 days and you can't close until day 31, the lender may very well say, "Sorry, you lose!" And you'll have to figure out some way of absorbing a higher interest rate and monthly payment.

The time you are allowed during the lock-in is usually negotiable. Most lenders will offer a short, 30-day lock-in of their best rates.

However, if you want 45 or even 60 days, you may find that lenders begin hedging. They don't want to give you their best rates. Rather, they will lock in a rate a little ahead of today's market. For example, if interest rates are currently at 7 percent, they will lock in at 7.25 percent. Your choice is to accept or go hunting for a more lenient lender.

> A mortgage broker can be very helpful when rates are rising. The representative can steer you to lenders that are willing to lock in their rates with little or no extra cost to you.

On some occasions, lenders may want a fee for the lock-in. Yes, they'll lock you in at today's rates, but it will cost you $75 or $150 or whatever.

What If You Lock In and Rates Drop Later On?

The lender expects you to go forward with the mortgage. You are locked in at 7 percent and rates drop to 6 percent. The lender will still want you to take out the mortgage at 7 percent.

Will you do it? Of course not. No sane person would. Lenders with common sense realize this and offer you their lowest rates at the time your deal closes. Others insist you take the lock-in.

> You're better off not locking in when rates are falling. You will have the benefit of the lower rate anyhow. If you lock in, you will have the hassle of arguing for a lower rate from the lender or having to go elsewhere.

Your mortgage broker should be smart enough to know which lenders insist on going forward with a lock-in even if rates fall. (If you're dealing directly with the lender, be sure to ask!) Then the MB simply switches you, as early on as possible, to a different lender. Voilà! You've gotten the benefit of the lock-in as well as the lower rate. (Of course, if you paid for the lock-in with up-front money, that's probably gone.)

What If You Lock In and
Rates Skyrocket?

That, of course, is why you wanted the lock-in the first place. If rates go up, you're sitting pretty. You've got the advantage of having the lower rate a month earlier. Of course, as noted above, you must close on time.

Another issue is whether a lender will honor its own lock-in. If rates goes up, the lender could lose big bucks by honoring its commitment. Will the lender take the loss or simply say, "Sorry"?

In most cases the lender doesn't really stand to lose anything. When the lender "locks in" a loan, it simply commits a small portion of an existing pool of lendable funds to pay for your mortgage. At some time in the past, that pool of funds was made available at a particular interest rate—say, 7 percent. And it's available at that interest rate for a short period of time, either until all the funds are loaned out or until 30 to 60 days pass. Even if rates go up, during that time frame, the money is committed at the stated amount.

A lender gets into trouble when it fails to lock in a part of the pool, but simply tells you that it has. Then if rates go up, the lender has to absorb the increase or leave you out in the cold.

This is a good reason to demand that the lender put the lock-in in writing. (Often the MB simply says, "Okay, you're locked in. Don't worry about it.") Worry? Get it in writing and be sure it's from the lender, not just the MB.

Of course, even if you have the lock-in in writing, what are you going to do if the lender doesn't honor its commitment? Sue the lender? Actually, you can complain to the Federal Trade Commission. That probably won't help in your individual case (the FTC usually investigates only patterns of abuse), but it may give you some personal satisfaction.

Just keep in mind that lock-ins generally are honored by the lender, but not necessarily by the borrower. They are a one-way sort of commitment that favors you. And in a field where so little favors the borrower, they are a great thing to have.

Power Tip 39
Don't Agree to a
Prepayment Penalty

Not long ago, prepayment penalties were the sort of thing you worried about when you paid off your car loan early. But few people considered them seriously when getting a real estate mortgage.

Actually, prepayment penalties on real estate loans date back to the 1940s. The bank gave you a real estate mortgage for a fixed number of years. If you paid it back early, you owed the bank a penalty—typically six months' interest. Back in the 1960s and 1970s, such penalties were written into every consumer mortgage.

More recently, when adjustable rate mortgages came into vogue—more precisely, when lenders stopped allowing borrowers to let others freely assume their mortgages—prepayment penalties were removed. Until the late 1990s virtually no consumer mortgages had them. Now, they are back.

Why Would the Lender Want
a Prepayment Penalty?

Why the new penalty? The snide comment is, "Because lenders think they can get it!" That's probably closer to the truth than most lenders would admit. However, the given reason is that with the plenitude of real estate loans now available, borrowers have taken to jumping from one loan to the next, always seeking lower rates.

Indeed, as interest rates fell during the mid-1990s, and many lenders incorporated their costs into so-called cost-free mortgages, borrowers began jumping from one loan to the next to save as little as a quarter point in interest. (From the borrower's perspective, why not? If you could get a lower interest rate, and resulting lower payment, without additional costs, why not switch?)

As a result, many lenders had to constantly rewrite their mortgages, always for lower rates. The additional expense of finding new borrowers and dealing with all the paperwork caused some lenders to throw up their hands and say, "Enough!"

Lenders began writing a prepayment penalty into the mortgage. Yes, of course, you could pay it off at any time. But, typically, if you paid it off before the end of three years, you had a stiff penalty—sometimes as much as six months' worth of interest.

Interestingly, as interest rates began to rise and the reason for instituting prepayment penalties (to keep borrowers from jumping ship) diminished, some lenders refused to remove the prepayment penalty. They liked the loyalty it inspired in borrowers, as well as the occasional money it brought in.

> Some lenders, particularly those offering second or "home equity" mortgages, found another way out. If the borrower sold the house, then there was no prepayment penalty. The penalty applied only if the borrower refinanced.

Check the Documentation and Ask Questions

The mortgage you apply for may have a prepayment penalty. Often the lender won't bring it up. And it may be buried deep in the loan's documentation. That means that if you don't want to pay, as you shouldn't, you should look carefully and ask.

Ask the lender's representative whether or not there's a prepayment penalty. If the rep says there isn't, make sure it's in writing.

If there is, get a copy of the clause in the documentation where it appears. Read it carefully. More than likely, you won't have to be a lawyer to understand it. It will typically say that if you pay off the mortgage before a certain period of time, a certain penalty will apply. The clause will give additional details—how the penalty is to be applied (as interest), and so on.

Since lenders won't allow you to change their documentation (you can't simply scratch out the offending clause), you'll probably have to look for a new lender. Do this early on. If you ask about the prepayment clause just as the deal's ready to close and the loan contains one, it's probably too late to do anything about it. You simply won't have time to find another lender, go through the whole financing process again, and save the deal.

What If the Lender Pays You for Accepting the Penalty?

Some creative lenders have taken to offering what amounts to a reward for borrowers who accept their prepayment penalty. They offer the borrower anywhere from $500 to $2,500 for letting the prepayment penalty remain on the loan.

Usually, however, the penalty is written in for more than the customary three years. Sometimes it extends on out to as much as 10 years. Further, if you do pay off early, you can be sure that the penalty is far and away higher than any reward you got up front. For example, you might get $1,000. But if you pay off the loan any time before six years have passed, you owe the lender $3,000.

Easy, you may be thinking to yourself. I simply take the money up front and then be sure not to pay off the mortgage for at least six years. It's a simple and quick way to pocket an extra grand.

The trouble is that few of us can predict the future accurately. It may turn out that because of a change in our finances, health, marital status, employment, or something else, we must sell the home before six years have elapsed. Now we are forced to eat that penalty. Suddenly that initial reward seems mighty puny.

Statistic: The typical family in the United States sells its home and buys a new one about every eight years.

Other Loans Are Available

It's important to understand that you don't have to accept a mortgage with a prepayment penalty. Plenty of lenders out there are more than willing to offer financing without that onerous clause. You just have to spend a little time looking.

Power Tip 40
Lower Your Interest Rate
by Getting a Shorter Term

Many factors influence the rate of interest a lender charges for a mortgage. These include the interest rate on 30-year bonds, the anticipation of coming inflation, and the demand for mortgages. None of these things do you have any control over.

However, one factor that you can control is the term of the loan. By adjusting it, you can lower the interest rate you have to pay.

Why Does the Term Affect the Interest Rate?

It has to do with risk. A typical home mortgage is for 30 years. If you lock in a fixed rate for that long a time, the lender could lose. After all, surely sometime during the next 30 years interest rates will rise above where they are when you get the loan. And when that happens, the lender suddenly has a subpar loan; its value declines.

Lenders know that most mortgages seldom last more than 10 years. Rather, borrowers refinance or sell, and the mortgage gets paid off. Nevertheless, in a typical loan, the lender's commitment is for the full 30 years.

Thus, if you are willing to take out a shorter loan, and decrease the amount of time the lender is at risk for interest rate movements, you can command a better interest rate. That's why 15-year mortgages, which are readily available, are often half a point or more lower in interest than a 30-year mortgage. It's also why adjustable rate mortgages (in which the interest rate fluctuates up or down, tied to a particular index) often start out at a much lower rate.

How Can You Get the Lowest Interest Rate?

It's simple. Give the lender the shortest term. If you get a mortgage for only three years (about the shortest currently available), you can often get an interest rate as much as a point lower than the market rate for 30-year loans. You've thus saved yourself 1 percent. On a $200,000 mortgage for three years, that's upward of $6,000.

But, you may be asking yourself, aren't the payments awfully high on a three-year loan? Indeed they are. On $100,000 borrowed at 7 percent for three years, the monthly payments on a fully paid back loan are an astounding $3,088—over 30 years they are only $665.

How Can You Afford the Payments?

The good news is that you don't have to pay the loan back in equal monthly installments. Rather, lenders are quite liberal about the payback requirements. You can pay the loan back as if it were amortized (paid in equal installments) over 30 years with a balloon payment at the end.

Be sure you understand the concept. The monthly payments are paid back as if there were 360 installments ($665 instead of $3,088 in our example above). However, the entire remaining balance of the mortgage is due at the end of year 3 (payment 36). You, in effect, have a balloon payment (where one installment is larger than all the others). Thus, you may indeed be able to afford the payments.

What Happens When the Mortgage Comes Due?

Remember, however, that the mortgage doesn't get paid off this way. Rather, you pay mostly interest for the time you have it and then, when the balloon payment comes due, the principal has to be paid off.

When that fateful day arrives, you usually have two choices. You can sell the property and pay off the balloon with the money you receive from the sale. Or you can refinance, perhaps getting another short-term, low-interest mortgage.

> It's a good idea to build automatic refinancing into a balloon mortgage, even if the refinancing is to an ugly, high-interest ARM. The idea is that in case you can't easily refinance (you've lost your job, are sick, or whatever), you still won't lose your house because the mortgage is due.

Are There Other Terms?

As an example, we've been using 3 years for the balloon payment. However, balloon mortgages are readily available for 5, 7, and 10 years as well. In the trade, they are referred to by their balloon and term. For example, a 30-year mortgage due in 7 is a 30/7 or due in 10, a 30/10. (A 15-year mortgage, however, is typically fully amortized, meaning that it pays off completely without a balloon after 15 years.) A mortgage with a guaranteed refinance to an ARM is also called a "two-step."

Most lenders will let you choose the balloon payment you want. Keep in mind, however, that the longer the term, the higher the interest rate. The shorter the term, the lower the rate.

Convertible Mortgages

There is yet another, related type of mortgage that can cut your interest rate. It works several ways. One of the most common forms is with an adjustable rate to begin. You get an ARM with a term of, for example, three years. However, at year 3 you have the option of converting it to a fixed rate loan at the then market interest rate, without additional financing charges.

For example, you borrow $100,000 on an ARM. Since ARMs give the lender flexibility in charging interest (the rate fluctuates with market conditions), it is typically for less than a comparable fixed rate loan. However, at year 3, you can convert to a fixed rate, at the then market rate. In this fashion you can, so to speak, have your cake and eat it to.

Another variety of the convertible gives you a certain window of opportunity to convert. For example, you might be able to convert at year 3 and at year 5. But at all other times you cannot convert. Thus, you have two opportunities to lock in a fixed rate. If rates happen to be low at year 3 or 5, you'll certainly exercise your option. If rates are high, you won't.

Another type of convertible automatically converts to an ARM after a certain time.

What should be clear from this discussion is that with all the types of mortgages available out there, by arranging the time frame, you can customize the loan to fit your particular needs.

Where Can You Get a Sophisticated Mortgage?

They may seem arcane, but sophisticated mortgages are readily available. Any lender or mortgage broker should be able to present a plethora of mortgage types with different time frames for you to choose from.

Power Tip 41
Don't Take Out 125 Percent Loans

Once two home owners had a dream, a fantasy. It was that a lender was so foolish as to lend them more than their property was worth. In that dream they would take the money and run.

In real life, today, it is possible to borrow more than your home is worth. In fact, loans for 125 percent of value have become commonplace. Unfortunately, in real life there's no way to take the money and run.

The temptation to borrow more than the value of your property, either when you purchase or when you refinance, is strong. After all, haven't we all heard that "cash is king"? If it is, why not simply take the cash and worry about the financing later?

There are several serious problems with 125 percent financing and we'll look at these shortly. However, first, let's be clear about what kind of loan this really is.

What Is 125 Percent Financing?

You may recall that all real estate financing is based on LTV (loan to value). That's the ratio of the mortgage to the value of the property. Traditionally, a mortgage was no more than 80 percent of value (80 percent LTV). That meant that if your home was worth $100,000, the maximum loan you could get was $80,000.

With 125 percent LTV, however, the maximum loan jumps to $125,000. Be sure you understand this clearly. If you wanted to sell your home on the market at the time of financing, the most you could get would be $100,000. Yet the lender is willing to give you $25,000 more.

Why Would a Lender Offer So Much?

It's all based on your good credit. If you have a great credit record, have borrowed before, and have paid back your loan, then the lender figures you'll do the same this time. In other words, with normal financing the property is the collateral. Here, your good credit is the basis for a substantial portion of the loan. Thus, the most common kind of 125 percent financing is part real estate loan and part personal loan.

This doesn't mean that you necessarily get two loans. It can all be combined into one loan. It's just that you pledge to pay off the mortgage personally, regardless of what happens to the property. This has some serious consequences.

What Is the Downside?

We all know the upside. You get cash out. You can use it to pay off existing credit card debt or other loans or simply to take a vacation or buy a boat. But eventually, the piper has to be paid.

When it comes time to sell your property, even if prices have appreciated, you will find that you have much less money coming back to you. Suppose you buy at $100,000 and get a 125 percent mortgage, or $125,000. Later, when prices have gone up, you sell for $150,000. Forgetting about the costs of sale (which can be substantial), instead of $50,000 in equity (the difference between what you bought for and what you sold for), you now have only $25,000 in equity. The other $25,000 went to pay back the mortgage.

This can be a real inconvenience, not to mention a financial downer. Consider, however, what can happen if you have to sell before prices go up. You might suddenly find yourself in a bind because of illness, job transfer, divorce, or any of a dozen other reasons. Suddenly you have to bail out of that property on which you obtained a 125 percent mortgage.

Only property prices haven't gone up. (They could have even gone down!) You suddenly discover that in order to sell, you have to pay the lender!

The property you bought for $100,000 may still be worth only $100,000. But you owe $125,000. When you sell, you're $25,000 short (not to mention closing costs and commission). What can you do?

You Are Responsible for the Debt

Remember, a 125 percent mortgage may be a combination personal and collateralized loan. Yes, property is the collateral for most of the loan. But the difference between what the property brings and the loan amount is your personal debt. It doesn't go away, nor is it canceled by foreclosure. You, personally, owe the money. If you can't pay, you could ruin your credit for a decade or more.

When you owe more than the property is worth, it's called being "upside down." In order to protect your good credit, you may be forced to keep the property and continue making payments. Or you must pay the lender back all that extra money you got when you obtained the mortgage. Neither scenario may be very helpful in your present situation.

> Another alternative in 125 percent financing is to ask the lender to transfer the mortgage to a new home you are buying. In other words, instead of having the mortgage on property A, which you sell, the lender now puts the mortgage on property B, which you buy. This, however, is entirely up to the lender, whose answer may simply be no.

There Are Potential Tax Problems

In addition to the dire results that could occur if you have to sell before the property appreciates, a 125 percent mortgage could lead to some problems with the Internal Revenue Service.

Most people who get a mortgage on their home plan to write off the interest. This is probably the only big tax deduction that the average person has left. And, given the size of the mortgage, the interest payment is typically quite large.

However, in order to be able to write that interest off, you must pass certain tests. In addition to the property being your primary residence (or second home), you must be liable for the debt (the mortgage is in your name), and the property has to be collateral for the debt. (There is also a limitation of $1 million in mortgage amount— $100,000 on a second or home equity loan.)

The problem with a 125 percent mortgage is that the property is not the entire collateral for the debt. How could it be? The debt is for more than the property's value. As a result, the IRS may determine that part (or even all) of the mortgage is actually a personal loan. And the interest on personal loans is not deductible.

What this means is that, depending on the IRS ruling, you may not be able to deduct all or even a part of the interest on that 125 percent home mortgage. This could have a very serious impact on your finances.

> It's been my observation that lenders of 125 percent mortgages have not done a particularly good job of explaining the potential tax consequences to their borrowers. I have seen statements such as "A portion of this loan may be deductible for tax purposes." That hardly explains the issue.

All of which is to say that 125 percent mortgages can be very dangerous items. My suggestion is that unless you are strapped for money and feel that you can't get a loan another way, you stay away from it.

Note: Because 125 percent mortgages may be a combination of personal and collateralized loans, they usually carry a higher interest rate than other mortgages. It's a "blended" rate. For example, if the mortgage rate is 8 percent and the personal loan rate is 14 percent, the 125 percent mortgage may carry a rate of 11 or 12 percent (depending on how much of the loan is considered collateralized and how much personal).

Power Tip 42
Don't Pay "Garbage" Costs

There are always costs associated with getting real estate financing. The lender wants to be guaranteed that you in fact own the title to the property, and that usually involves getting a lender's policy of title insurance. It also involves running an escrow to handle the transfer of funds to you and the mortgage/deed of trust to the lender.

Then there are documents that have to be recorded (recording fees), notary fees, credit checks, an appraisal, and a few other costs, all of which are reasonable and necessary. And all of which you have to pay.

However, in recent years some lenders have chosen to tack on additional fees that are neither reasonable nor necessary. These extra charges have earned the name "garbage fees."

Why Do Lenders Add on Garbage Fees?

From the lender's perspective, the purpose of garbage fees is to raise the yield of the mortgage. This is a subtle point, but worth exploring.

Every mortgage has a "yield," which is usually different from its interest rate. The interest rate is what you pay and on which your monthly payments are based. The yield is what the mortgage returns to the lender. How can the two be different?

It's easy. Consider points. You borrow $100,000 at 8 percent and two points. What's your interest rate? If you answered 8 percent, you're right. What's the lender's yield?

That's more difficult to calculate. It's handled like this. Instead of receiving $100,000, you actually get only $98,000.

Remember those two points? (Each point is worth 1 percent of the mortgage.) When you pay points, they are subtracted from the loan amount. Thus, you're in fact borrowing only $98,000, yet paying interest on $100,000. That's roughly equivalent to a yield of 8.25 percent.

Think of it this way. The monthly payments on $100,000 at 8 percent are about $734 a month (for 30 years). However, you borrowed only $98,000. Paying $734 a month on $98,000 is roughly equivalent to having a 8.25 percent loan.

All of which is to say that the lender can increase the yield on the mortgage without increasing the interest rate. This is done, in no small measure, to make borrowers think they are getting a better deal than they really are.

For example, when rates are high, a lender may offer interest at a lower than market rate, but high points. The yield to the lender (the combination of points and interest rate) may still be at market. But because the stated interest rate is lower, borrowers think they are getting a bargain.

In recent years, when rates dropped down to historic lows, lender stopped charging points at all. Rates were so low that borrowers didn't worry about them. However, as rates stabilized, then increased, borrowers were again looking and comparing the interest rates they were charged. They began to balk at the higher rates.

In the past, the simple solution was to just lower the rates and charge more points. But by this time, borrowers had become used to paying little to no points.

So, being the creative folks they are, lenders began throwing in all sorts of extra charges. Since borrowers paid little attention to these costs, lenders got away with them. And these extras, the new garbage fees, increased the yield of the mortgage.

Today, when you borrow, you will typically have both points and garbage fees. What's important to understand is that points are negotiable, as we'll see in a later tip. Garbage fees are too, although most borrowers don't realize it.

How Do You Get Rid of Garbage Fees?

You have to ask the lender to simply remove garbage fees. Once some lenders realize you are aware of these fees, they will simply take them off. Other lenders, however, may refuse. Your choice is to vote with your feet, by taking your business elsewhere.

This means that you have to recognize and challenge garbage fees at the beginning of a transaction, when you first select your lender. It's usually too late to make the discovery at closing. If you try to do something then, the lender may simply say, "Sign the papers or forget about the mortgage." If you refuse to sign, it may be too late to go through the paperwork of getting another lender. If you balk, it could cost you the deal, possibly your deposit, and even a legal challenge from the sellers.

Doing it at the beginning isn't hard. When you first apply for a mortgage, a lender is required to give you an estimate of your costs. The Real Estate Settlement Procedures Act (RESPA) demands this. Even though RESPA is almost never enforced, the vast majority of lenders do make the effort to come up with a fair estimate.

Read the statement over carefully. Look for garbage fees. Challenge them. (Check Power Tip 50 for a list of fees.)

Power Tip 43
Trade Points for Interest and
Vice Versa

If interest is what you pay a lender for the privilege of borrowing money, then what are points?

Frequently, they are interest too. In a sense they are prepaid interest, although that brings up a whole can of worms with the IRS and that's a separate issue.

A point in mortgage finance is generally described as 1 percent of the mortgage amount. Thus, if you borrow $100,000, one point equals $1,000. Two points equals $2,000; $2\frac{1}{2}$ points, $2,500; and so on.

Lenders frequently tack on points as a way of offering a higher-yield mortgage at a lower interest rate. For example, a mortgage without points might have an interest rate of 7.5 percent. However, if you pay two points, that rate might drop down to 7.25 percent. By paying points, you can affect the interest rate of the mortgage. (See Power Tip 42 for an additional explanation.)

In the past, lenders were quite inflexible regarding points. They would offer, for example, a loan at 8 percent and three points—and that's it. Take it or leave it.

Recently, however, the relationship between points and interest rates has become more widely understood by consumers. As a result, some savvy consumers have been demanding, and getting, more flexibility. Today lenders are frequently willing to trade off points against interest rate.

> Trading off points against interest rate means that if you are willing to pay more points, you can get a lower interest rate. Pay a higher interest rate, and you can get fewer points.

Why Would You Want to Trade Off
Points and Interest Rate?

It all depends on your situation. Let's say that you're short of cash when you want to purchase your home. You've got to come up with the down payment, plus the closing costs, plus the points. But that's stretching things too thin.

So you negotiate with the lender for a slightly higher interest rate in exchange for not paying any points at all. Since points are cash, you've effectively reduced the amount of money you'll have to come up with to close the transaction.

Of course, with that higher rate, you'll owe more interest and your monthly payments will be a bit higher. But perhaps it's worth it to you in order not to have to come up with additional cash.

On the other hand, you may be having trouble qualifying for a mortgage or, for whatever reason, you want smaller payments. So you go to a lender and negotiate a lower interest rate by paying more points up front. You might agree to pay, for example, five points in order to get a 0.5 percent reduction in interest rate, and the resulting lower payment.

While lenders won't negotiate all trade-offs, today many will negotiate reasonable adjustments.

> You have to watch lenders closely to make sure they don't try to take advantage of you. They may, for example, raise the interest rate higher than necessary to make up for the points they eliminate. Or they may add more points than is justified by a lower interest rate.

What's the Ratio of Points to Interest Rate?

Of course, knowing the ratio of points to interest rate is how you tell whether you're getting a fair deal or getting cheated when the terms are adjusted. However, it's important to understand that there is, in fact, *no single ratio* between points and interest rate. Rather, it gets back to a matter of yield.

A certain combination of points and interest rate will produce a given yield on a mortgage. If done fairly, the yield will remain the same regardless of how the points or interest rate is adjusted. Whenever the yield goes up as a result of a trade-off between points and interest rate, you know you're being taken to the cleaners.

How do you know the yield? You can ask the lender (preferably before you start negotiating the trade-off). You can calculate it yourself (again see Power Tip 42). Or you can have a real estate agent, escrow officer, or other loan officer calculate it for you. Some calculators on the Internet also do a good job here. Try www.eloan.com.

What Is a "Buy-Down"?

A buy-down is simply another way of saying that you are paying extra points to get a lower interest rate.

Buy-downs occur mostly in the sale of new homes when interest rates are seen as being high. (Sometimes sellers in resales will offer buy-downs as well.) Builders feel that they can't get enough buyers because the high rates are keeping would-be purchasers from qualifying. Lower the interest rates, however, and more people qualify to make the purchase.

So the builder goes to the lender and says something to this effect, "I'll pay you points up front, if you will give me a below-market interest rate." Since the yield on the mortgage to the lender is the same, most will agree.

Thus, when you ask the builder about purchasing a new home, the builder can boast about offering below-market interest rates. That means lower payments, easier loan qualifying.

Be aware, however, that the buy-down may be limited. Frequently it's done in stages. For example, in a frequently used buy-down, the first year the loan is 3 percent below market, the next year 2 percent, the third year 1 percent, and then it's back to market rate. Be sure you understand the steps, if any, being used in a buy-down given you by a builder. The reason is that as the interest rate rises, so too will your payments. (If your payments are capped—not allowed to rise—you may have a negatively amortized loan, meaning that the excess interest is added to principal, which results in your owing more each year than the year before!)

The money for a buy-down has to come from somewhere. If the builder, for example, is paying $10,000 extra in points to the lender in order to get a lower interest rate, it only stands to reason that all or at least a significant part of the money is being passed onto you in the form of a higher price for the home.

Power Tip 44
Use Creative Financing
to Your Advantage

Two decades ago "creative financing" was the hottest buzzword in real estate. More recently, however, the term has been looked upon disparagingly. Indeed, some have gone so far as to say it is more aptly called, "stick-the-seller financing"!

The major reason for the fall from acceptance of creative financing was the push to get into real estate with no money down in the mid-1980s. At that time, a good number of unscrupulous buyers asked sellers to finance their purchase of a property. Then the buyers would "trash" the real estate. They would rent it out, collect the rents, and not pay back the seller's financing. They hoped to quickly resell at a profit. Failing that, they simply let the home go into foreclosure. The big loser, of course, was the seller.

However, just as it's important not to throw out the baby with the bath water, so is it important not to throw out the technique of creative financing just because it was once abused. Indeed, it can be an extremely useful tool to help you, the buyer, purchase a home that you might otherwise not be able to buy.

What Is Creative Financing?

Creative financing refers to having the seller, instead of an institution, give you a mortgage. Rather than go to a mortgage broker or get a loan from a bank, you persuade the seller of the home to finance all or part of the sale. Along the way you can get some terrific benefits.

Benefits to Buyer of Creative Financing

1. *Little to no qualifying.* Sellers typically want only a simple credit report on you. They are often willing to forgive many problems that institutional lenders do not overlook, including bankruptcy and previous foreclosures.

2. *Lower than market interest rate.* Often it is possible to negotiate a favorable interest rate, sometimes significantly less than the going market rate for mortgages.

3. *Higher LTV.* Sellers may give you a higher loan-to-value ratio than institutional lenders. Indeed, in some cases they may finance 100 percent of your purchase. (This is what gave creative financing a bad name in the first place.)

4. *No points or excessive fees.* Unlike an institutional lender, a seller doesn't normally charge points. In addition, the only cost is usually the charge for drawing up the documents and recording them, typically $100 or so.

5. *Quick action.* Since the seller gives you the financing, there are no committees that need to approve the loan, no delays waiting for underwriting, and no holdup with funding. The money is the seller's equity in the property and it's ready to go when you are.

You Can Get In When Other Lenders Turn You Down

Perhaps the biggest advantage to most buyers of creative financing is the fact that it can allow you to purchase a property when you are otherwise turned down by institutional lenders. Remember, sellers don't scrutinize your credit history, income, and assets nearly as much as do institutional lenders. And they are usually willing to forgive a great deal.

You might go to a conventional lender—a bank, for example—and learn that with your credit history or your income, you simply can't get a mortgage big enough to cover the home you want. Does this mean you can't buy? No, it simply means that now is the time to turn to creative financing.

A word of caution, however. When a lender turns you down, it's because you don't meet that lender's profile for a successful borrower. As noted earlier, today lenders use extremely sophisticated profiling to decide who can afford a mortgage and who can't. If the lender says you can't, you ought to consider carefully if the lender might not be correct. You don't want to get in over your head and not be able to make the payments, eventually losing the property to foreclosure. Unfortunately, there are far more foreclosures in creative financing than with conventional mortgage lending practices.

> The reason that sellers are frequently willing to turn a blind eye toward credit problems or low income is that they are motivated to sell their property. They want the deal to go through as much as you do. Thus, often when they should exercise caution, they jump forward, just to get rid of the property.

How Does It Work?

In the simplest to understand form of creative financing, the seller finances the entire purchase for you. How can the seller do this? Let's assume you find a seller who owns a house free and clear—no mortgage on it.

Normally in a purchase, you would offer to put up a small down payment and then get financing for the balance from an institutional lender. However, here you propose to put up the down payment and then have the seller give you a mortgage. Perhaps you'll put 10 percent down and the seller will give you a 90 percent mortgage.

Why would sellers do this? There are many reasons. The most common occurs when the sellers are older. They might have been planning to put the money from the sale in the bank and live off the interest. You can offer them higher than bank interest (yet still lower than market rate mortgage interest) in a secure investment. They might jump at it.

More likely, however, the sellers still owe something on their home—they have an existing first mortgage. If that first mortgage is assumable (as is the case with older FHA and VA loans), you take it over and have the sellers give you a second mortgage for the difference between it and the selling price, less whatever you put down.

Alternately, you might get a new low first mortgage and have the sellers give you a second mortgage for a higher amount, thus reducing your down payment. This is sometimes a useful strategy when you can't qualify for a big first mortgage, yet don't have enough cash for a big down payment.

In all the above cases, it's important to understand the mechanics of the deal. The seller normally doesn't give you any money. Rather, part or all of the seller's equity in the property is converted to a mortgage. Instead of giving the seller cash for the equity, you now give the seller paper.

Will It Really Work?

It's important to understand that creative financing works best in normal to cold real estate markets. When the market is hot and deals are being made right and left, sellers are usually loath to carry back financing. They really don't have to. Why accept your "creative" offer when more traditional offers are coming in? Thus, unless the seller wants to carry back paper (as in the case of an older seller who needs the income), you probably won't be able to do much creative financing in hot markets.

Power Tip 45
Get an Asset-Based Loan

Are you one of those people who doesn't have much credit but has a lot of money, stocks, or bonds?

When I say doesn't have much credit, I don't necessarily mean that your credit is bad. Rather, it could be that you simply haven't established much credit. You pay cash for most things and generally don't borrow. You may not even have a credit card. When you buy a car, you pay cash. As a result, you simply don't have a lot of credit. On the other hand, over the years you've accumulated a fair amount of wealth.

Now you want to buy a home and, because of the price, you simply can't (or don't want to) pay cash. Rather, you want to get a mortgage. However, because you haven't established a strong credit history, the usual lenders won't offer you a mortgage. Does this mean that you're out in the cold, unable to purchase the home of your dreams?

Not at all. You're the perfect candidate for an asset-based mortgage.

What Is an Asset-Based Mortgage?

In the case of a traditional mortgage, the basis for lending you the money is threefold: You have strong credit, proving that you will endeavor to pay back the loan. You have a strong income, meaning you will have the funds to make payments. And you are putting a sufficient down payment into the property to show that you are a serious buyer and simply won't walk away if something unfortunate (such as a layoff, illness, or divorce) happens in the future.

In the case of an asset-based mortgage, none of the above apply. Rather, the basis for offering you the mortgage is that you have a lot of money in the bank. For example, you want a mortgage of $200,000. You happen to have $200,000 (or more) in the bank. You pledge the money in the bank as security for the mortgage. Virtually the next day the mortgage is yours. You've got it, no other questions asked.

Think this type of financing is unusual? Not at all. It's exactly the kind of financing that was initially proposed to allow Bill and Hillary Clinton to purchase a home in New York State. A wealthy friend was to put up over $1 million in cash in the bank, enabling the Clintons to obtain an asset-based mortgage for the same amount of money. (The arrangement wasn't used because of the political issues it raised.)

Why Would You Want an Asset-Based Mortgage?

There are a lot of reasons for getting an asset-based mortgage. Here are three of the most important.

Reasons to Get An Asset-Based Mortgage

1. *You can't get regular financing.* For whatever reason, lenders won't give you a mortgage. With asset-based lending, there's no problem.

2. *You want a better interest rate.* Typically with an asset-based mortgage, you get a much lower than market interest rate. After all, you have the perfect collateral.

3. *You don't want to touch your assets.* Instead of cash, your assets might be stocks or bonds. You don't want to sell these, yet you want the mortgage. So you pledge them. Be careful here, however, because if their market value declines, the lender could ask you to pledge more.

Who Offers Asset-Based Mortgages?

You'll have to sidestep the regular mortgage lenders here. You're unlikely to get a mortgage broker or even a mortgage banker to help you with an asset-based loan.

On the other hand, any commercial bank should be willing and able to take care of it. After all, it's simply a partly uncollateralized loan, and that's what banks offer all the time.

What If You Need Your Assets?

This is always the thorny question with asset-based mortgages. You've pledged your cash, stock, bonds, or whatever as collateral. Now, suddenly, you have a need for that money. Perhaps there's a buying opportunity in the stock market too good to pass up. Or maybe you want to fund your children's education. Perhaps you've been sick and there are medical bills. Can you get your assets out?

Yes—and no.

It depends to a great extent on the lender and its flexibility. If you've made payments regularly on the asset-based mortgage for years, the lender may simply release all, or more likely a portion, of your assets. This isn't common, but it can happen.

On the other hand, by now perhaps you've paid down the mortgage amount and the lender can convert from an asset-based mortgage to a conventional mortgage (in which the property itself is the sole collateral). You'd get your money out.

There may be additional solutions. Each case is different and you'll have to check with your lender. Nevertheless, getting an asset out once it's been pledged remains the biggest sticking point with these type of mortgages.

Power Tip 46
Get a Mortgage on
Another Property

Are you "land poor"?

This phrase refers to a person who owns a lot of property, but who has little cash. It often occurs when people try to play Monopoly® in the real world, building their net worth by buying ever more homes. The negative cash flow, even when people rent out the properties, becomes overwhelming, absorbing most of their income. Indeed, in some desperate cases the properties are described as "alligators," eating up their owners.

In most cases, however, people with multiple properties simply have a lot of real estate. And often they want to buy more, either another home for themselves or another rental property.

However, because they are so overexpanded, it becomes difficult for them to get financing for their new purchase. Lenders may refuse to consider a new mortgage.

> When you have rental property, your rental income does not count 100 percent toward your mortgage and other expenses, for financing purposes. Lenders discount rental income by 10 to 20 percent, assuming that over time you'll have vacancies and the associated costs of repair and fix-up.

When this happens, it may be time to look at financing a different way. Instead of getting a new loan on the property you are purchasing, consider a loan on a property you already own.

What Kind of Loan Can You Get on an Existing Property?

That depends on the existing financing. Very often, if there's already a first mortgage on the property, you can get a second mortgage. If it's the home in which you reside, it can be in the form of a home equity loan. Typically these are for up to 80 percent of the LTV. So if you have an existing mortgage of, say, 40 percent of LTV, you can get a second mortgage for another 40 percent. (Remember,

LTV stands for loan to value—40 percent LTV on a home valued at $100,000 is $40,000.)

These mortgages, sometimes called equity-based loans, may allow you to purchase another property that you could not otherwise afford.

Can You Get a "Blanket" Mortgage?

I'm sure you've heard the advertisements on radio and television plugging home refinancing. The idea is that you get one big loan and use it to consolidate your debt, paying off a bunch of little loans. You can do the same thing in real estate.

If you have several properties, each with a separate mortgage, you can get a blanket mortgage that covers them all. In this case it's a mortgage that lists each property as collateral.

What Are the Advantages of a Blanket Mortgage?

Here are the primary advantages of a blanket mortgage.

Advantages of a Blanket Mortgage

1. *You can get a lower interest rate.* Overall, the rate on the new blanket loan may be less than the combined interest rate of all the small mortgages. Of course, this depends on when you refinance. However, if you do it during a drop in market rates, you can often get a very favorable blanket rate at the same time as eliminating higher-rate older, smaller loans.

2. *You can get more money out.* If you need money to buy another property, it can be difficult to get enough by trying to do a lot of little financing. This is particularly the case if no one property you own has enough equity to handle a mortgage of the size you need. All together, however, it may be a different story. Further, while lenders may balk at two or three different small finances, they may be happy to do one blanket loan for you.

3. *You have only one payment to make.* While this may not be a big consideration, it does mean that at the beginning of each month

there's a lot less bookkeeping for you. On the other hand, that one payment will be a whole lot bigger than any of those little ones.

What Are the Drawbacks of a Blanket Loan?

Besides the one big payment, noted above, the biggest drawback of a blanket loan is that you stand to lose *all* your properties if you get into financial trouble. Perhaps you have a job loss, or an illness, or a spate of bad tenants who won't pay and won't move so you don't have rental income.

With a bunch of little properties, you might be able to make the payments on most and sacrifice one or two. With a blanket loan, they are all at risk. Don't make the payments and the lender takes them all back.

> Lenders will sometimes tie blanket loans to your creditworthiness. If for whatever reason you begin to have a lot of bad credit, they may call the loan. It's something else to consider.

Where Do You Get a Blanket Loan?

This is customized financing. It requires multiple appraisals, escrows, title insurance, and so on. While a few mortgage brokers might be sophisticated enough to handle the blanket loan, it's more likely the purview of a good commercial bank.

Power Tip 47
If You're Self-Employed, Get
a Low-Doc, No-Doc Mortgage

People who are self-employed have the hardest time getting real estate financing. Lenders often don't want them as borrowers.

The reasons that lenders don't favor self-employed people as borrowers are threefold.

Why Lenders Don't Favor Self-Employed People

1. *It's difficult to establish income.*   If you work for someone else, it's easy to determine whom you work for and how much you make. You simply show up with a paystub that says it all. (This can be confirmed with your employer.) On the other hand, if you work for yourself, how does the lender know what your true income is? The usual method of determining such income is to ask you to bring in the last two years of your federal income tax returns. Even so, that doesn't really establish what you're making during the current year. (Lenders will often ask for a profit/loss statement, but it's usually not verified.)

2. *Too often the borrowers exaggerate their income.*   If you work for someone else, the lender can ask your employer for a statement of how much you make. It's easy, clean, and simple. If you work for yourself, however, it's much too easy (from a lender's perspective) to exaggerate or even lie about your income. It's harder for the lender to be certain of what you make.

3. *The borrowers tend to be financially unstable.*   Lenders feel that if you work for someone else, even if you get fired, you can always get another, similar job. If you work for yourself, however, any number of things from illness to a change in the market can drive you out of business. And once you've lost your business, you may not easily be able to create another. The loss of income will result, eventually, in your defaulting on your mortgage. Whether any of this is true makes little difference; it's the way most lenders think.

> Recently, lenders have achieved the ability to confirm on computer, directly with the IRS, the 1040 forms turned in to verify self-employed income. Verification virtually eliminates the false 1040 that lenders dread and that some unscrupulous borrowers have tried using.

The Problem With "Other" Income

Besides lender bias, as noted above, probably the biggest problem with getting traditional financing for some self-employed people is that their true income is "under the table." This means that it's part of the cash economy.

While the legal issues involved are between the self-employed individual and the Internal Revenue Service, it's a different story with a lender. Generally speaking, as far as a lender is concerned, if you can show sufficient before-tax income, you should be able to get financing.

The problem with "under the table" income is that it doesn't show up on federal income tax forms. In other words, there's no way to document it. (This is another good argument for declaring and paying taxes on all your income.)

What's the Best Way a Self-Employed Person Can Get a Mortgage?

If you, as a self-employed person, attempt to go through the regular mortgage procedure, you may find that you're up against a whole series of roadblocks, any one of which may be enough to keep you from getting a mortgage. You may simply not have worked enough years on your own to satisfy a lender's requirements. Or you may not be able to show enough income. (Yes, you may be making it, but if it doesn't show up on Schedule C of Form 1040, as far as the lender is concerned, it isn't there.) Or you may be in a field that the lender feels isn't solid enough to ensure that you'll be able to continue working satisfactorily into the future.

Therefore, it may behoove you to do a little end-around play. Instead of going through the regular mortgage procedure, look into Low-Doc, No-Doc mortgages.

What Are Low-Doc, No-Doc Mortgages?

The difference between Low-Doc, No-Doc and other mortgages is primarily the documentation required to secure the loan. As we've been discussing, with a traditional mortgage, you have to prove through documentation exactly how much income you have, that you are employed, and so on.

With these types of mortgages, you simply have to sign a statement swearing that the figures you give to the lender regarding employment and income are accurate. The lender takes your word for it. You don't submit the 1040 forms or other documents. Instead, you get your loan.

> With a No-Doc loan (rare these days), no documentation of any kind is required. With a Low-Doc loan, some documentation is required. It can include income tax statements and other documents such as savings or checking account statements.

Is it really that simple? No, of course not. It never is. When Low-Doc, No-Docs first came out, they were seen as a godsend to the self-employed, who had trouble documenting their income. However, early abuses by borrowers who exaggerated or outright lied about their income, then went into foreclosure after defaulting on their mortgages resulted in lenders pulling back.

More recently, as lenders have begun making a better effort to screen their borrowers, we have seen a comeback of the Low-Doc variety. As of this writing, the No-Doc loan remains difficult to find.

> With Low-Doc, No-Doc loans you can get into serious trouble if you ever default on the mortgage. At that time, the lender may demand to see proof that you didn't lie when you first made your application. If you cannot demonstrate your veracity, you could be in serious trouble with the IRS for lying on an application to a federally insured lender (as most modern mortgages are).

Are There Any Drawbacks?

Generally speaking, Low-Doc, No-Doc mortgages carry a higher than market interest rate. That might translate into higher points as well. The premium is to compensate the lenders for the added risk.

Who Offers Low-Doc, No-Doc Mortgages?

It really depends on when you look. At certain times, no one in your area may offer them. At other times, all lenders have one or more different Low-Doc products available. Your best approach is to check with a good mortgage broker.

See the checklist for *Get Lenders to Work for You* on pages 207–208.

6
Easier Closings

Power Tip 48
Have Sellers Pay Your Costs

Often those who are not familiar with real estate transactions over-look closing costs when buying a home. That's a mistake, since the closing costs can be almost as much as the down payment!

There is a way, however, to reduce those costs. And that's to have the sellers pay them! Before we see how that's done, let's take a look at what those costs actually are.

When you're buying, you'll probably have some, if not all, of the following costs to pay.

Typical Closing Costs

- *Points.* Points are paid to a lender as part of securing your mortgage.

- *Escrow charges.* Sometimes there are two escrows, one for the house and the other for the lender.

- *Title insurance charges.* Usually the sellers pay title insurance, but it's according to local custom. You may need to pay. In addition, you very likely will need to pay for special lender's title insurance.

- *Recording fees.* Fees charged to record your deed and mortgage.

- *Attorney's fees.* You must pay any attorney you hire for the transaction.

- *Other fees and costs.* Some additional fees are necessary to any real estate transaction. Others may simply be garbage. (See Power Tip 42 for more details.)

- *Recurring costs.* These include taxes, interest, and fire/home owner's insurance premiums.

The total amount can run to many thousands of dollars. And the question becomes: Can these fees be reduced in some way?

The answer is yes, maybe. It all depends.

Why Would the Sellers Pay Your Costs?

Given a choice, sellers wouldn't pay your closing costs. After all, would you pay the sellers' costs, which may be significantly higher than yours because of the broker's commission?

However, you can include the closing costs as part of the negotiation process. Depending on how flexible the sellers are (and how good a negotiator you are), they may be induced to pay all, or at least a part, of your costs.

Keep in mind that in a very hot market, it's unlikely that the sellers will pay any of your costs. Why should they? If you don't buy the home, there are probably half a dozen other buyers waiting in line to purchase, and some of these buyers may be offering better deals than you. However, in a normal to cold market where you're the only buyer in sight, it's a different story.

How Do You Get the Sellers to Pay Your Costs?

It's important to remember that closing costs are usually cash that you must come up with. If the sellers are willing to foot this bill, or a part of it, it's cash saved from your pocket. When buying a house and coming up with a down payment, you may find that cash is in short supply. Therefore, you may be highly motivated to have the sellers pay your costs.

You may be so highly motivated, in fact, that you are willing to pay a slightly higher price for the home. For example, the house may have an asking price of $210,000. You offer $195,000. The sellers come back at $205,000. You agree to the sellers' figure, provided they pay $5,000 of your closing costs.

From the sellers' perspective, you are actually offering to split the $10,000 difference. You'll come up to $200,000 if the sellers come down to that figure (by paying $5,000 of your closing costs). Some sellers might readily agree. You've bought yourself a home for $205,000; however, of that amount, $5,000 will go to pay your closing costs. It's probably not a bad deal, in that you've just converted $5,000 that you would otherwise have to pay in cash to a slightly increased price.

It's all a matter of negotiation. Some sellers will be happy to pay in order to make the sale. Others will have trouble understanding what's going on and will be hesitant to do it. Still others will simply be obstinate and refuse.

Of course, there are other ways to negotiate the same sort of arrangement. For example, I recently sold a home for which the buyers insisted that I pay $3,000 of their closing costs. Apparently they were short of cash and needed extra money to make the deal.

Realizing that I would jeopardize the sale if I refused, I agreed to pay their closing costs. On the other hand, I refused to repair a deck that had significant dry-rot damage and that they wanted repaired as part of the deal. They agreed to forgo the deck repair (which would probably have cost me around $3,500) and the deal was made.

The point here is that almost anything can be negotiated as part of the deal. If you want or need to get extra money (pay less in closing costs), consider getting the sellers to pay it for you. Give them something they want and they often will go along.

You can run into problems when the sellers pay your closing costs. For example, if the sellers pay interest on your mortgage or your share of prorated taxes, who gets to deduct it for income tax purposes—them or you? Further, lenders may balk at having sellers pay some of your recurring costs.

To avoid this sort of problem, it's best to have the sellers pay only "nonrecurring" costs—fees that occur one time only during the closing of the deal. These include such costs as title insurance and escrow charges.

Power Tip 49
Finance Your Closing Costs

Another method of reducing the cash you have to come up with at closing is to have the money folded into the financing. In short, you have the lender pay your closing costs. This is similar to having the buyer pay (see the previous Power Tip), except that instead of affecting the price, it affects the financing.

Here's how it works. During the negotiations between you and the sellers, you offer to put 15 percent down. Let's say the house you've agreed on has a price of $100,000, so you're going to come up with $15,000 and get an $85,000 mortgage.

However, you have a total of only $15,000 in cash and there's another $5,000 in closing costs. The total cash you need to come up with is $20,000. You're $5,000 short.

So you propose the following. The price will remain the same except that, instead of an $85,000 mortgage, you'll secure a $90,000 mortgage. And instead of putting $15,000 down, you'll put only $10,000 down. As far as the sellers are concerned, it should make no difference at all. It's a cash sale to them of $100,000 whether the money comes from the lender or from you.

As far as you are concerned, however, by increasing the mortgage amount, you have an extra $5,000 left over, which you can now use to pay your closing costs. You have, in effect, financed the closing costs.

What Are the Pros and Cons of
Financing the Closing Costs?

You've now got a bigger mortgage and slightly higher monthly payments. Also, you've got less equity—$10,000 as opposed to $15,000. So when you resell, you'll get less out of the property.

On the other hand, you've been able to make a deal that you otherwise did not have the cash for. Had you not financed the closing costs, you would have been $5,000 short.

Will the Lender Go Along?

Maybe. It all depends on how much financing you can get. In our example, you went from an 85 percent LTV (loan to value) to 90 percent. Assuming that you qualify for a 90 percent loan, the lender will probably be happy to go along. After all, the lender is in the business of lending money and you've just asked to borrow more.

On the other hand, if you're already at your limit, stretching may be difficult. Let's say you're already at a 90 percent loan and now you want to go to 95 percent. That last 5 percent can make a big difference. A lender may have to get you a different kind of loan with a higher interest rate. And you may have difficulty qualifying for it.

> The traditional down payment is 20 percent. Today, 10 percent financing is common. But lower than 10 percent often requires special consideration by lenders. Although there are 95 percent loans available (indeed 100 percent LTV loans are available), the qualifying is stricter and lenders require PMI (Private Mortgage Insurance) on all loans of more than 80 percent LTV. This adds about another 1/2 percent in interest.

This, of course, is the beauty of getting preapproved. You can sound this all out with the lender at the time and be ready to go when you make your offer. (See the very first Power Tip.)

Are There Any Alternatives If the Lender Won't Do It?

There are always alternatives. The question is: Do you want to take them?

You can try to have the sellers pay your closing costs as described in the previous Power Tip. Or you can try to get additional financing.

For example, in addition to the first loan that you are getting from a lender, you might go to a different lender and try to secure a second mortgage. Let's say you have a first mortgage of 90 percent LTV and the lender won't go higher. You go to a different bank or credit union and secure an additional 5 percent to pay your closing costs. Now your total loans (first and second) are up to 95 percent and you've got the cash to make the deal.

Be aware that today many institutional lenders look not only at LTV (loan to value), which we've discussed here and elsewhere, but also at CLTV (combined loan to value). This is the total of all your loans to the value of the property. Getting secondary financing of 5 percent on a 90 percent first mortgage would give you a CLTV of 95 percent, which the first lender may not like. As a consequence, that first mortgage lender may now refuse to give you the 90 percent LTV loan.

Lenders generally do not mind financing the closing costs. Indeed, in most cases it just means getting a higher LTV and, as a consequence, a higher loan with more interest to the lender.

However, lenders do want to see that you have enough cash on hand to make whatever down payment is agreed upon, pay the closing costs, and have at least a month or two in reserve in case of an emergency. And, as noted above, they may balk if they feel you are getting too much financing overall on the property.

Power Tip 50
Avoid Hidden Buyer's Fees

Nothing sours your good feelings toward a home you're purchasing more than to discover that you're being asked to pay all sorts of fees that you hadn't anticipated. You thought you had a deal, plain and simple. Only, as you get your escrow papers, you discover that it really wasn't so plain or so simple. There are hidden extras (also called garbage fees), sometimes dozens of them. What are you going to do?

What Are the Hidden Extras?

Hidden extras will vary from deal to deal. Here are some of the more creative types that I've found over the last few years. These typically appear in the RESPA (Real Estate Settlement Procedures Act) good faith estimate of costs that you get when you apply for a mortgage. Or they may also show up in the escrow payment documents that you get shortly after opening escrow. You may discover additional costs when you get your closing documents at the time you sign off on the deal. (See also Power Tip 42.)

Hidden Extra Fees

1. *Application fee.* You can't get a mortgage without an application. But you can fill out an application without paying a fee. Indeed, you shouldn't have to pay a fee in this situation.

2. *Assumption fee (too high).* If you are assuming an existing mortgage, the lender will probably charge a fee for handling the paperwork. The fee is usually around $100. Any more than this and it's probably not a reasonable charge.

3. *Commission (not your agent or collected twice).* Paid to the real estate agent, the commission shouldn't normally appear on the buyer's estimate of cost sheet. It could, however, if you used a buyer's agent or agreed to pay part of the seller's agent's fee. However, be sure that the agent isn't collecting twice, once from you and a second time from the seller!

4. *Closing review fee.* Here the lender is charging you for going over the closing documents to be sure they all comply with the lender's requirements. It's sort of like being charged by a new car dealer for going over the purchase agreement to be sure you've signed in all the right spots. Outrageous!

5. *Courier Fee (unnecessary deliveries).* A courier is a special messenger. Sometimes in a transaction it becomes necessary to send documents from point A to point B in a timely fashion rather then via regular mail or overnight via express mail. If you need a document delivered during the day, a courier may be necessary. And if that's the case, then you should expect to pay.

However, once in a while the courier is just the person who transports the loan documents from the lender's office to the escrow company and back. It may be just across the street! Yet the charge may be in the hundreds of dollars. It's something else to watch out for.

6. *Credit report fee (too high).* The lender charges for a credit report. This fee usually is under $50, often $25 to $35. It is a normal and customary fee. You have to pay it, unless the lender agrees to absorb the cost, which some highly competitive lenders do. Beware, however, of charges of $100 or more for this report.

7. *Discount points (more than agreed).* This is a one-time charge. Each point is equal to 1 percent of the loan. Points are used to adjust the yield of the mortgage to correspond to market conditions. Be sure that you aren't paying for more points than you agreed to when you first signed on for the loan. Be aware that lenders often add points to compensate when the interest rate is below market.

8. *Document drawing/signing fee.* This is a new twist. It's a charge from the escrow company for creating the instructions that are needed for the escrow. And it sometimes includes a fee for having someone give you the documents and watch you sign them! It's as if you're being charged twice—once for the escrow and a second time for doing the escrow's work.

9. *Document preparation fee.* This is the most common of the hidden extras. It's the charge from the lender for drawing up your loan documents. It's sort of like going to a store and buying a refrigerator. Only one of the costs of the purchase is a charge for having the salesperson write up your order. No store would ever get away with it. But lenders sometimes think they can.

10. *Escrow charges (fees too high).* The escrow is an independent third party who accepts all the monies, gets the deed prepared, and then handles the actual closing of the transaction. In the Midwest and West this service is performed by an escrow company (often the same company that issues the title insurance). In some states on the East Coast the function is performed by an attorney. There is a fee for the

service and you should expect to pay it. However, some escrows are significantly more expensive than others. Shop around. You normally aren't bound to use any particular escrow company. You can use the one that gives you the best price.

There may be a separate "lender's escrow" in addition to the escrow you are using to purchase the property. This may be necessary if the financing involves other properties or is in some way complex. Otherwise, it is a garbage fee paid either to the escrow company or to the lender.

11. Fire insurance (fee too high).   You will be required to provide fire and hazard insurance policies to protect the lender. Typically you must pay for these policies at least one year in advance into escrow. However, the policies are written for three years and some insurers require that all three years be paid in advance. Be sure to shop around for the best rates.

12. Impounds (too many months collected).   If your mortgage was for more than 80 percent loan-to-value ratio, you will probably be required to impound taxes and insurance. Setting up the account requires a "cushion." What this means is that the lender will collect a couple of months of taxes and insurance from you in advance in order to get the account started, and then pay them when due. If more than this amount is set aside, it's not only not kosher, it may be illegal and you could have rights against the lender.

13. Impound setup.   Some lenders charge a separate fee for setting up the impound account and yet another fee for administering it. These are also usually garbage fees, since the setup should be a normal part of doing business. Challenge them.

14. Lender's attorney's fee.   Of course, the lender is going to have an attorney. That's the person who will be drawing up the documents for you to sign and who will be sure that everything is legal, so that the lender can foreclose within the law if you fail to keep up the payments. But you shouldn't have to pay for it separately. It's a cost of doing business that the lender should pay. Challenge this fee.

15. Lender's title insurance (fee too high).   Most lenders require a separate, more comprehensive, and more expensive policy of title insurance. This is frequently required because of underwriting. You'll simply have to pay it. Just be sure the cost is reasonable. Shop around.

16. Mortgage insurance premium (only if you actually have mortgage insurance).   If you have an FHA loan or a loan for more than 80 percent

LTV, you'll have to pay for insurance. For an FHA loan, this has to be paid all in advance into escrow. For private mortgage insurance, the amount may be for several months in advance, to cover the payment in the event you default on the mortgage. However, on occasion a lender will put insurance on even though your loan doesn't need it. Challenge the charge.

17. Origination fee. This is a charge to cover the lender's administrative costs in processing a loan. It is standard with FHA government-insured loans. But it shouldn't be there for conventional loans.

The origination fee shouldn't be confused with another garbage fee sometimes called the "setup" fee. It's often a few hundred dollars that lenders charge. For example, a particular mortgage might be two points plus $350. The $350 is the setup fee. It goes to pay for initiating the processing of the loan.

To my way of thinking, there is no justification for this fee. The lender is getting the interest; that should be sufficient. If there are other administrative costs, the lender should cover them and the interest rate should be adjusted accordingly. However, almost all lenders do squeeze in a few hundred dollars as a way of getting additional money when obtaining a mortgage. Challenge the fee, but don't expect the lender to remove it every time.

18. Underwriting review fee. If you get a conforming loan, it means that the lender has to have the underwriter (Fannie Mae or Freddie Mac) review and approve it. The underwriter charges the lender for this service. However, traditionally this fee was always picked up as a cost of doing business by the lender. Only recently have lenders begun trying to pass it on to you, often with an additional hefty charge for preparing it. Resist it.

19. Warehousing fee. Lenders sometimes charge for the interest on the mortgage between the time the lender makes it available to you and the time the deal actually closes—usually equivalent to two or three days' worth of interest. It's strictly garbage. These days the lender can keep the money in an interest-bearing account until the moment it is used. There's no need for you to pay interest on it until you receive it. Challenge this fee.

20. Writing and managing documents fee. A new charge that goes by many names such "Escrow Management," or "After Offer Processing." It is charged by agents as a way of increasing their income without increasing their stated commision. I wouldn't pay it.

Keep in mind that there are many legitimate charges. For example, expect to pay $250 and upward for an appraisal. Legitimate loan processing fees could cost as much as $500. Then there are the basic fees, noted above, for escrow, title insurance (if you happen to be paying it and not the sellers), lender's title insurance, tax service, prorations, and other costs relative to your type of transaction. If you're not sure if the fee is normal and necessary, check with your agent or your real estate attorney.

In addition to the costs listed above, there could be additional charges that may or may not be reasonable. You'll have to use common sense here or check with your real estate attorney.

Who Charges Extra Fees and Why?

As you can tell, most of the extra hidden fees come from the lender. The rest usually come from the escrow company.

The reason they are charged is to increase their income from your purchase, without actually increasing the basic costs. A lender, for example, may want to give you a highly competitive interest rate. That means both a low rate and low points. But the money it costs the lender may be high. So how can the lender make you the loan, yet still collect a profit? The answer may be these hidden extras. The lender's profit may in large part reside in them.

The same holds true with escrow companies. They want to have competitive pricing, yet they need more income. So they create hidden extras. I don't know about you, but I would much rather pay a higher basic fee and be up front about it than have hidden extras thrown in.

What Can You Do About Them?

Remember, the time to challenge lender's fee is when you first get your good faith estimate. If you don't like a fee, ask the lender about it. If the explanation isn't adequate, ask that the fee be removed. If the lender refuses, consider finding a different lender.

The real problem, of course, is getting rid of the hidden extras. Can you do it? How do you do it?

The answer seems to be vote with your feet. If you discover that a lender or an escrow company is charging a hidden extra, complain about it. And if the offending party won't take out the fee, drop out and look elsewhere. There's no shortage of lenders or escrow companies.

What's important to understand, however, is that you must do this early on. It's too late to try to switch loans, or escrow companies, when the deal is ready to be signed. An attempt to do so, in fact, could cause such significant delays that the sellers might balk and refuse to go along. In that event your deal, your deposit, and even more could be in jeopardy.

Rather, be sure to ask and receive a complete breakdown of costs from both the lender (you should receive an estimate anyway under RESPA) and the escrow company at the time you open escrow and begin securing financing. That way, if you don't like what you see, you'll have time to look elsewhere.

See the checklist for *Easier Closings* on pages 208–209.

7

When Buying a Brand New Home

Power Tip 51
Be First in Line

Get in line and stay in line whenever new homes are in short supply. In some areas of the country (such as parts of Northern California and New York State), there is actually a shortage of buildable land. Jobs are concentrated in relatively small geographical areas and people cram to live close in.

In those areas, builders know they can sell anything they can build. The problem, however, is that most of the easily buildable land has already been developed. What remains is farther away than most people want to travel or is on land that has water problems, is steep, or is otherwise difficult to build upon.

Nevertheless, the demand drives developers to move forward and when they do, because of the difficulty in building, they often construct a relatively few houses. The result is many, many buyers for few new homes. Competition for new homes gets particularly difficult in an overall hot market.

Scout the Area

If this is the situation near where you live, then I suggest you spend some time early on scouting out the area to see where new building is taking place. This means spending a few weekends traveling the byways, particularly areas that have not yet been developed. It also means going down to the building department and asking if any new tracts have recently been approved nearby. Then check it out.

Don't be put off by the fact that there are no houses above ground, yet. Construction takes place fast. Look for roads and utilities being put in, lots leveled and ready for construction, or foundations being poured.

Typically there will be a fence around these projects with many "keep out" signs. These serve two purposes: They keep "civilians" (those not involved in construction work) from poking around and accidentally hurting themselves. They also discourage criminals from coming in and stealing construction materials—unfortunately, a serious problem at any building site. Nevertheless, there will almost surely be a phone number on the protective fence telling you whom to call for information on purchasing the homes.

On a construction site you can always stop a worker and ask for the foreman, who can usually direct you to the developer. You want to make contact as early as possible.

Get the Facts

In a tight market, the developer will receive all sorts of inquiries regarding the new homes. However, smart developers won't commit to sales until they have several homes up that potential buyers can look through. There are good reasons for this.

First, the developer doesn't really know when or even if the project will fly until at least a few homes are up. Second, as anxious as potential buyers may be, they really don't know if they want to buy until they can see the homes. Thus, signing people up early on and taking deposits (which must be refundable in most cases) becomes an exercise in wasted time and effort.

What you are likely to learn from the developer is only the following:

How big the homes are going to be.

What the likely price range will be.

When the homes are expected to go on sale.

Where the tract will be. (Sometimes it's spread around and not just where you began looking.)

You have to supply the *why*—namely, letting the developer know that the reason you're calling is that you're interested in buying. If the builder is putting together a list of potential buyers to call when the project is completed, be sure your name is on that list.

Stay on Top of It

It might be just a few weeks until the homes are ready to be offered for sale, or it might be several months. Either way, don't rely on the developer to call you, regardless of whether your name is on a list. Keep calling back, at least once a week.

Yes, this will turn you into a pest. But it will also let the developer know you are keenly interested. And it will let you know how much progress is being made.

In the meantime, chances are that a few models will be completed. Go through these carefully. Decide exactly which model you want with what options. Be specific. Write everything down.

Also, recheck your financing. Be sure that your preapproval is still good (see the first Power Tip) and that you have enough financing and down payment to cover the home and the closing costs. Get an extension on the date and have your preapproval letter ready.

When the developer finally lets you know that on a certain date the sales office will open to accept purchase offers, if the market's hot and there are few new homes in the area, move quickly.

Get There Early

Let's say that the developer lets you know that the following Sunday morning at eight o'clock, the sales office will open to accept purchase offers. Should you show up at eight o'clock on Sunday? Not if you want one of the new homes in a tight market.

Developers can handle crowds of buyers who want to purchase homes in two ways. The first is to establish a written list months in advance. The developer takes a deposit and puts you on the list. When the homes are ready, the developer calls to let you know your home is ready.

The problem with this system, for the developer, is that some people are only casually interested. On the off chance that they may want the home, they put up a small, refundable deposit. These people may have changed their minds or already bought elsewhere. On the other hand, as the list gets long, other, more serious buyers may turn away, fearing they have little chance of getting a new home with so many names ahead of them.

Thus, the early list can become inefficient, from the builder's perspective.

The second method is to take those who come to the sales office on the day the properties are initially offered on a first come, first served basis. This means that only those truly interested will be there.

Typically the builder has someone call those who left their names; you might get such a call letting you know when the sales office will open. Or you might discover the date and time from one of your regular weekly calls.

The trouble is that all the other would-be buyers will also know. And since the early bird usually does get the worm, some of the more determined people will get there early. They will stand in line waiting outside the sales office to be the first let in.

How early will they get there? If the office opens at eight o'clock, will they be there at seven? Actually, in many really tight markets I have seen people show up anywhere from three to seven days early! They bring along a cot or a sleeping bag and have family supply them with food and drink and occasionally spell them so they can take care of life's other necessities.

In some cases there can be some pushing and shoving, and fights can break out over positions in line. In short, it can (and in some cases has) develop into a real free-for-all.

To keep order, most developers will pass out number tags to those in line. The first gets number 1, the second number 2, and so on. How many are passed out depends on how many homes are for sale. If there are 50 homes and 300 potential buyers, the developer may pass out only 100 or 150 numbers, assuming that from that group at least enough qualified buyers will be available to gobble up all the new homes. Those without tags can still wait in line, but they must realize that their chances of getting a home are remote.

Once you get one of these numbers, you don't have to remain in line. You can go home and just show up on the given date and time (Sunday at eight o'clock, in this case). Then you'll be ushered in to be told the terms of the purchase in order of the number you have.

Be Prepared to Pay More

Developers are no one's fools. As the line of potential buyers gets longer, the price gets steeper—up to certain limitations. In a true supply/demand situation, the developer could simply auction the homes off to the highest bidder. (And this is occasionally done.) In most situations, however, the price is set by the lender's appraiser, who determines what the homes are worth—their current market value. It simply becomes impractical for buyers to get financing above that limit, at least not until a higher price level is established. (The alternative is to ask for more cash from buyers. However, developers well know that the one thing even the most eager buyers rarely have is more cash. Thus, a demand for more cash could simply mean the houses might go unsold.)

Nevertheless, appraisers are not immune to trends in market conditions. A line of determined buyers in front of a sales office will make any appraiser reexamine his or her figures. And a reevaluation upward could, and sometimes does, occur between the time the builder tells you what the price of the homes will be when you are looking and what the asking price is when it comes time to make the actual purchase.

The rule is to always figure it will cost more and be prepared with additional financing and down payment, as may be necessary.

Be Ready With a Hefty Deposit

The developer may demand a big deposit, perhaps $10,000 (more or less depending on the price of the homes). You may be required to put this up in the form of a cashier's check.

In addition, if you've already agreed on a specific lot and floor plan, the developer may have already filled out your purchase offer for you. It may specify the price, the down payment, the amount of financing, even the lender, although the developer most likely won't be able to enforce these terms. The conditions of purchase may also be spelled out. You may be told that you either take it or leave it. Your only options are to insert any upgrades you may wish to purchase at an additional expense.

On the other hand, the developer may realize that everyone is different. The amount of down payment and financing may be negotiable, as may be some terms such as when the escrow is to close and when you will move in. Obviously, the greater the demand for the few homes, the more leverage the developer will have—and the fewer options you will have.

Of course, you can always exercise your option to walk. If you find the price, financing, or other terms onerous, you may want to simply pick yourself up and move right on out. There will be other opportunities—there always are.

On the other hand, you may be willing to settle for a pretty stiff deal if you feel this is just the right property for you. And you may be influenced by the housing market. If prices are moving up 5 percent or more per year in your area, you may feel that no matter how difficult a deal the developer is pushing, you can always live there a year or two and then sell for a whopping profit.

> Keep in mind that a 5 percent appreciation on a home, when all you've put in for a down payment is 10 percent, amounts to a 50 percent profit for you!

What You Should Watch Out For

A Price That's Higher Than the Appraisal. The developer may be hoping for a second, higher appraisal, or may be anticipating that you'll come up with more cash to cover the difference between the appraised market value and the inflated asking price.

Financing Through the Builder's Lender That's Costlier Than Financing You Can Arrange. Your lender may be asking only 8 percent. But the builder's lender may want 9 percent. You'd be paying 1 percent a year more ($1,000 on every $100,000) if you go with the builder's lender in this case. On the other hand, your lender probably won't accept the builder's lender's appraiser. This means that if you go with your lender, you'll need to get a new appraisal (which may or may not equal the asking price). It will probably take anywhere from a week to a month, depending on how busy appraisers are. The developer may simply refuse to sign the deal with you because of the additional time you are taking (and because there are others waiting in line behind you, if you decide to bug out).

Onerous Financing Terms. The builder's lender may only offer an adjustable rate mortgage, whereas you want a fixed rate. There could be added points. (A point is charged by the lender as part of the closing costs—one point equals 1 percent of the loan value.) There could be many add-on garbage costs to you such as fees for the lender's attorney or for "warehousing" the money (keeping it ready for you until the deal closes).

The Wrong Lot, Floor Plan, or Upgrades. If you draw lucky number 1, you should be able to pick any lot, floor plan, or upgrade. But if you pick number 49 out of 50, your choices will be severely constrained. Instead of the view lot, you may get the lot next to the water tank. Instead of the single-story three-bedroom, you may get the two-story four-bedroom. Instead of granite countertops, your floor plan may call for only white ceramic tile. The possibilities go on and on. Even though you may be one of the lucky ones to get a home, it may not turn out to be the home you dreamed of.

What Can You Do About It?

Try to Negotiate. You may have some leverage on your side. If you're preapproved and fully qualified to get the financing, have the down payment and closing costs in hand, you are a top buyer. Yes, there may be another 10 or 20 people in line behind you, but a buyer who is ready, willing, and able to purchase is a fairly rare commodity and the developer knows it. Throw a little weight around. Let the developer know you're a top buyer. It may win you some concessions (less likely on price, more likely on terms). On the other hand, if you're a marginal buyer, be very careful when negotiating. Get your back up straight and refuse something and the developer may not hesitate to say, "Next!"

Walk. As noted earlier, if you don't like what you're given, go somewhere else. Yes, you may not get a house today, but all markets turn around eventually. Perhaps renting for a time would be a viable alternative, until prices settle down, more homes get built, or your finances improve.

Try to Sell Your Position. You don't really like the lot, house, upgrades, price, or terms. But you are number 3 in line and there are 150 people behind you ready to buy 50 houses. Maybe you should resell to someone else. You might be able to do this in several ways:

1. Simply sell your high number in line to someone else. Maybe number 145 would pay $100 or even $1,000 to have number 3. There's a tidy profit for only time spent. (Be sure the builder hasn't registered names and allows selling of positions.)

2. Resell the home while it's in escrow. Before you complete the deal, you may find another buyer who's willing to purchase from you for more. You begin the purchase process, then resell before your deal closes. This, however, is called "double-escrowing" and

is generally considered both unethical and illegal, unless the other party (in this case, the developer) knows about it. And if the developer knows about it, chances are he or she will want that profit you stand to make and will try to find some clause in your purchase agreement to prevent you from reselling.

One way to avoid reselling problems is to purchase the property under both your name and another name to be designated. If the builder agrees (and he or she may if you have a big deposit you stand to lose), you won't have any problem substituting another buyer, but you may still be required to meet all the terms of the agreement, including the time for completion of escrow. Check with a good lawyer for the correct language to use in your state.

3. Complete the purchase and then immediately resell. If the market's really hot, and if you get the names of disappointed buyers in line, you could pull this off and pocket a tidy sum, all within a few weeks. Just beware of all the hidden costs in a real estate transaction from escrow and title fees to loan prepayment penalties. It could cost you 10 percent or more as part of the turnaround.

In a tight market in an area that's been developed out, you may have to show initiative and creativity to get the home you want.

Power Tip 52
Buy Homes in Stock

Some sage advice when negotiating the price of an automobile is to always try to purchase a car that's on the dealer's lot. In-stock cars cost the dealer interest each month and they clog up the lot, taking up space that should be used for the next batch of models that are arriving. That means that you're likely to get a better price on them from the dealer, who wants them out of there. Besides, if the car's on the lot, you can test it out and see what you're getting. If you buy a car that's yet to be built and delivered by the manufacturer, you won't know until it arrives if you really like the color or if it drives well.

Something very similar applies to new housing. In the old days (before the housing recession of the early 1990s), developers would put up huge tracts of homes. Sometimes as many as 500 homes or more were built at a time, just waiting for buyers.

Of course, the builder was paying heavy interest on the construction loans of these homes. And until those loans were paid off, it was difficult for the builder to get new construction loans to start additional homes. In other words, the builder wanted them out of there.

As a consequence, if you looked at the models and said that you'd like to buy the home on Randall Street that was already constructed, the builder might be very anxious to deal with you. On the other hand, if you said you wanted to put a deposit down on the property on Conrad Street, to be completed sometime in the next six months, the builder would be less enthused about dealing. Yes, he or she would certainly take your deposit. But no, almost just as certainly there wouldn't be any chance to negotiate a lower price.

The Market Condition Rules

Of course, whether the builder is willing to negotiate at all on the price is primarily a factor of the market condition. If the market is hot with houses selling as fast as they can be put up, chances are the only price will be full price.

On the other hand, in a normal to cold market prices become negotiable. During the early 1990s when the housing market crashed, many builders were left with huge tracts of unsold homes. With prices falling, buyers fled and builders were threatened with insolvency because of the interest payments due on all their unsold properties. Needless to say, they were very anxious to cut buyers a deal, any deal, to get out of the property. This meant reduced price (when possible—the property couldn't really be sold for less than the builder had put into it). It also meant terms advantageous to the buyer, such as a bought-down interest rate or no closing costs.

In a way, it was the best of times and the worst of times for buying a new home. Times were good because of the deals you could make. They were bad because the house you bought today might be worth less tomorrow.

By the turn of the century, however, the market had once again switched gears. Housing sales were up and builders were again putting up tracts of homes, though not as large as before. And with lots of buyers around, it was more difficult to negotiate a better deal.

Nevertheless, in all but the hottest markets—where people were waiting in line to buy homes (see the previous Power Tip)—if you were going to get a deal on a new home, your best bet remained negotiating for a house already under construction.

Other Advantages to Buying Already-Built Homes

You never know what a housing development will look like until it's built. The look of the street changes when homes go up on bare land. Landscaping, or the lack of it, can make a huge difference. Simple things such as the color of the homes, their presentation to the street, and the size of the setback in front (the distance from the home to the curb) also count.

Even inside the home, the newly constructed unit may differ markedly from the model home. And options that you don't choose (mirrored doors, open ceilings, extra loft area, and so on) can change the whole feel of a home. All of which is to say that you're better off being able to actually walk into and see what you're getting.

This is not to say that people don't successfully put deposits down on homes, wait months for them to be built, and then like what they get. It can and does happen. But why take the risk when there are already-built homes out there?

Be sure that any deposit you put down on an unbuilt home is fully refundable. You want to be able to back out of the deal if your dream home ends up looking like a nightmare.

Power Tip 53
Get Upgrades, but Don't Buy
Them Separately

I like to use analogies from the auto field because they are so applicable to new homes. When buying a car, get all the upgrades you want thrown into the price—you'll get them at discount. If you wait until after you've negotiated the price, then you'll end up paying full retail for any upgrades. Something very similar happens with homes and upgrades.

Should You Get Upgrades?

In almost all cases, you'll want the upgrades. If the home comes with wall-to-wall carpeting, chances are the chosen carpets are thin, have a loose weave, and are put down over inexpensive padding. Since nothing adds warmth and luxury to a home like carpeting, you'll want to get this upgraded.

If a room has floor-to-ceiling mirrors, it's probably because the room is small and the mirrors make it appear larger. Of course you'll want the mirrors.

If there's a choice of countertops in the kitchen, unless you're lucky and the basic countertop is of high quality, you'll want the upgrade. It will make a big difference when working in the kitchen. And you'll get more bang for your buck when it comes time to sell.

However, upgrades are typically very expensive when you're buying a new home.

When they learn of the cost of upgrading, many buyers want to forget buying the upgrade through the builder and get their own instead. This, however, may be impractical. Usually a home can't be financed until it is completed, which means, for example, all floor covering. Thus, the builder can't sell you the property without the carpeting. On the other hand, if you pay for carpeting before you buy, and then for some reason you don't go through with the sale, you probably won't get all your money back. Thus, getting your own carpeting when buying a new home is simply unrealistic.

Often the builder will set up a model room with examples of all the upgrades available. Or the builder may open a "design center" displaying all the possible upgrades. You go to the room or the design center and make your choices. However, the prices may be extraordinarily high, much more than you'd pay if you bought something very similar on your own.

The same may hold true for any changes in construction that the builder allows or for other items that are in addition to the base price of the home.

> Builders often offer only a handful of different configurations or changes to the basic plans. (Some offer none.) The reason is that changes involve getting new approvals from the building department as well as new costs and financing, which the builder may only be able to guess at. It simply is too much effort and too costly for most builders to honor individual requests for changes.

The way to get the upgrades at a more reasonable cost is to include them in the price of the home you're buying. Just as you negotiate over price, negotiate over upgrades. Yes, you'll buy Plan 395—the "Tropicana"—*if* the builder will throw in upgraded carpeting, countertops, and floor-to-ceiling mirrors. If not, then you'll look elsewhere for a more complete package.

Will the Builder Negotiate Upgrades?

Sometimes builders say that their hands are tied when it comes to upgrades. Because of considerations with building departments and financing, only certain upgrades were chosen. And because of the narrow selection, the prices are high. The builder hasn't got any room to negotiate.

If you believe that, there are a lot of telemarketers who would like to talk with you.

Let's return to the analogy of selling a car. The typical markup of a new car is around 11 percent. That's the amount a dealer makes based on the msrp (before incentives, which the manufacturer gives to get the dealer to move certain models). However, the typical markup on upgrades is actually around 50 percent, sometimes more. Indeed, some dealers make more money on the sale of upgrades than they do on the sale of the car! (I recently bought chrome wheels for a new car. Their retail was $1,500. However, when I had them thrown in as part of the deal, the dealer gave them to me at "cost," $600. I believe the actual cost was far less even than that.)

Something similar operates with builders. Yes, there is the cost of running the design center. However, often the option manufacturers (carpet sellers, tile people, and so on) will help defray those costs. And in some cases a group of builders in an area may all get together to pay for the design center.

If the market isn't too hot for the homes, chances are the builder will be willing to negotiate. If so, you can suddenly find that the price of the upgrades, when calculated into the overall purchase price, drops significantly.

When you buy upgrades, always try to have them included in the negotiation over the price. Chances are you'll save oodles of money that way.

Tit for Tat

Every item that's added to negotiations becomes a bargaining chip. If you throw in upgrades, then expect some other area where you may have to give. For example, you insist that the lot be fenced, an upgrade. The builder says, "Okay, but you'll have to come up with the cash down and closing costs in 30 days." That's much sooner than you wanted. But to make the deal, you agree. As with everything else in real estate, there's always going to be some give and take. And you would be foolish to believe that you'll get everything your way all the time.

See the checklist for *When Buying a Brand New Home on* pages 209–210.

Checklists

Chapter 1: Plan Before You Purchase

1. Are you "preapproved"?   ☐
2. Is your preapproval from a legitimate lender?   ☐
3. Are you looking in neighborhoods with "high percentile" schools?   ☐
4. Have you checked out the "Graffiti Index" of the neighborhood?   ☐
5. Is shopping handy?   ☐
6. Is there good access to transportation?   ☐
7. Are there few if any rentals nearby?   ☐
8. Are you using a "buyer's agents"?   ☐
9. Do you know how to avoid paying a buyer's agent fee?   ☐
10. Is there a good HOA in the neighborhood?   ☐
11. Have you prepared a real estate map of where you want to find a home?   ☐
12. Do you know how much you can afford to pay?   ☐
13. Do you know where you want to buy?   ☐
14. Have you evaluated the market?   ☐
15. Do you have a plan of action?   ☐

If you didn't check any of these questions, you overlooked or skipped some portion of Chapter 1. A quick reread will help you get off to a better start.

Chapter 2: Strategies for a Hot Market

1. Have you personally canvassed your chosen neighborhood?   ☐
2. Have you weeded out ineffective agents?   ☐
3. Are you prepared to wait out an evasive seller, if necessary?   ☐

4. Are you willing to offer more than the selling price? ☐

5. Do you know enough to stay clear of multiple-offer auctions? ☐

6. Do you understand the perils of a multiple counteroffer? ☐

7. Are you willing to do the legwork to be the first offer in? ☐

8. Do you understand the risk of buying "sight unseen"? ☐

9. Do you understand the pros and cons of "as is" homes? ☐

10. Are you willing to take on the work of a fixer-upper? ☐

11. Can you calculate how much a fixer will really cost? ☐

12. Can you identify the "out of favor" home? ☐

13. Can you identify which homes will eventually go up in value? ☐

14. Are you willing to talk to an FSBO?

15. Do you know the arguments to use on an FSBO? ☐

16. Are you willing to take a "backup" position? ☐

17. Do you know the right contingencies to put into a backup position to protect yourself? ☐

18. Can you risk making a cash offer? ☐

19. Will you be able to sleep nights if you do? ☐

20. Do you understand how "liquidated damages" work? ☐

Buying into a hot market is one of the toughest tasks any buyer can undertake. If you're not able to check off all of the above questions, then you need to bone up on strategies and tactics.

Chapter 3: Tactics for Successful Offers

1. Do you understand why you should never give the sellers more than 24 hours to accept your offer? ☐

2. Do you know how to respond to an agent who wants you to give the sellers more time? ☐

3. Do you understand what a "contingency" is? ☐

4. Do you know which contingencies you should
   have in your offer? ☐

5. Will you turn contingencies into deal points? ☐

6. Will you watch out for frivolous contingencies? ☐

7. Do you know why you should start with a small deposit? ☐

8. Are you willing to raise your deposit later? ☐

9. Do you understand that your deposit is always at risk? ☐

10. Do you understand why you need to have an
    inspection? ☐

11. Do you understand the real purpose of disclosures? ☐

12. Are you willing to use the disclosures and the
    inspection report as negotiating tools? ☐

13. Do you know where to find highly motivated sellers? ☐

14. Are you willing to push a highly motivated seller? ☐

15. Are you willing to trade terms for price? ☐

If you're going to get a good deal, you have to be assertive. You
also have to know where the deal points are. If you're not sure and
have not checked off some of these questions, you will find it helpful to reread Chapter 3.

Chapter 4: Profiting in a Normal or Cold Market

1. Will you look at more expensive homes than you
   can afford? ☐

2. Are you willing to make offers on them? ☐

3. Do you know what a low-ball offer is? ☐

4. Are you willing to risk a low-ball offer to get a
   better price? ☐

5. Do you know the risks and rewards of foreclosures? ☐

6. Are you willing to take the time required to find
   good foreclosure properties? ☐

7. Do you know what an REO is? ☐

8. Are you willing to confront banks in order to get info on REOs? ☐

9. Are you willing to bid at an auction? ☐

10. Do you understand the perils of buying at auction? ☐

11. Do you know what an auction "reserve" is? ☐

12. Do you understand what an upside-down seller is? ☐

13. Are you willing to profit by helping an upside-down seller? ☐

14. Do you know what a "short sale" is? ☐

15. Are you willing to pressure a lender to give a seller a short sale? ☐

Many of the strategies and tactics here will work in most markets. They work best, however, when the market is cold or at least not highly active. If you're not sure how or when to apply them, recheck Chapter 4.

Chapter 5: Get Lenders to Work for You

1. Are you a prime borrower? ☐

2. Are you subprime? ☐

3. Do you know where to find a mortgage if the normal institutional lenders won't give you a loan? ☐

4. Do you know the best time to get a fixed-rate loan? ☐

5. Do you know the best time to get an ARM? ☐

6. Do you understand what "adjustment periods," "caps," and "steps" are? ☐

7. Is a "balloon" mortgage advisable for you? ☐

8. Do you know the benefits of a biweekly mortgage? ☐

9. Are you willing to try electronic lending? ☐

10. Do you know how to find out if you qualify for a VA loan? ☐

11. Are there advantages to taking out an
    FHA loan? ☐

12. Do you know the benefits of a home equity mortgage? ☐

13. Are you willing to pay the costs of a "jumbo"? ☐

14. Do you understand the difference between a
    "mortgage broker" and a "mortgage banker"? ☐

15. Do you know how to avoid up-front fees? ☐

16. Do you know the power of the lock-in? ☐

17. Do you know when to avoid it? ☐

18. Do you know how to avoid a prepayment penalty? ☐

19. Do you understand the pitfalls of a "125 percent"
    mortgage? ☐

20. Can you list most of the "garbage fees"? ☐

21. Is a buy-down advantageous to you? ☐

22. Are you willing to try "creative financing"? ☐

23. Do you know the arguments to use on a seller to
    get creative financing? ☐

24. Do you understand how an asset-based
    mortgage works? ☐

25. Are you willing to risk your assets? ☐

26. Do you understand "blanket" mortgages? ☐

27. Do you understand borrowing on property A to
    buy property B? ☐

28. Is a low-doc, no-doc loan for you? ☐

Good financing is the key to getting a good deal in real estate. If you had trouble with the above questions, it will pay you to look back at the Power Tips in Chapter 5.

Chapter 6: Easier Closings

1. Do you know why sellers might be willing to pay
   your closing costs? ☐

2. Do you understand what closing costs are? ☐

3. Have you found out how much typical closing costs are in your area? ☐

4. Do you understand how to "finance" your closing costs? ☐

5. Do you know how to structure a deal so the closing costs can be financed? ☐

6. Do you know what to do if a lender balks at financing the closing costs? ☐

7. Do you understand that there are hidden fees that buyers are often charged? ☐

8. Have you looked at the list of typical hidden fees? ☐

9. Do you have arguments to use to avoid paying them? ☐

10. Do you know when to check for the hidden fees? ☐

Closings can be a breeze, or they can be terrible. It all depends on how prepared you are. And being prepared means that you know what to anticipate. If you're not sure, recheck the Power Tips in Chapter 6.

Chapter 7: When Buying a Brand New Home

1. Do you know why you should be first in line to buy? ☐

2. Have you scouted the area for new-home developments? ☐

3. Have you ascertained the types of homes that will be built? ☐

4. Are you checking back regularly with the builder? ☐

5. Are you willing to up your price to get a better-located home? ☐

6. Are you ready with a big deposit? ☐

7. Are you watching out for an overpriced new home? ☐

8. Are you ready to "walk" if the builder tries to deal you a bad price, bad terms, or a bad house? ☐

9. Do you know the advantages of buying an
   already-built new home?   ☐

10. Have you checked out the market to see if it favors
    you or the builder?   ☐

11. Do you want upgrades?   ☐

12. Are you willing to pressure the builder to include
    upgrades in the overall price?   ☐

Buying a new home can be a wonderful experience, unless you pay too much or get something you really didn't want. If you feel uncomfortable about the purchase, reread the Power Tips in Chapter 7.

Glossary

If you're just getting introduced to real estate, you'll quickly realize that people in this field speak a different language. There are "points" and "disclosures" and "contingencies" and dozens of other terms that can make you think people are talking in a foreign language.

While this should be a tiny stumbling block that can be quickly overcome with occasionally humorous results (over terms you don't understand), too often the real consequences are that you get confused and perhaps even act (or fail to act) on something important. Therefore, it's a good idea to become familiar with the following terms, which are frequently used in real estate.

Abstract of Title: A written document produced by a title insurance company (in some states an attorney will do it) giving the history of who owned the property from the first owner forward. It also indicates any liens or encumbrances that may affect the title. A lender will not make a loan, nor can a sale normally conclude, until the title to real estate is clear as evidenced by the abstract.

Acceleration Clause: A clause that "accelerates" the payments in a mortgage, meaning that the entire amount becomes immediately due and payable. Most mortgages contain this clause (which kicks in if, for example, you sell the property).

Adjustable Rate Mortgage (ARM): A mortgage whose interest rate fluctuates according to an index and a margin agreed to in advance by borrower and lender.

Adjustment Date: The day on which an adjustment is made in an adjustable rate mortgage. It may occur monthly, every six months, once a year, or as otherwise agreed.

Agent: Any person licensed to sell real estate, whether a broker or a salesperson.

Alienation Clause: A clause in a mortgage specifying that if the property is transferred to another person, the mortgage becomes immediately due and payable. (See also **Acceleration Clause.**)

ALTA: American Land Title Association. A more complete and extensive policy of title insurance and one that most lenders insist upon. It involves a physical inspection and often guarantees the property's boundaries. Lenders often insist on an ALTA policy, with themselves named as beneficiary.

Amortization: Paying back the mortgage in equal installments. In other words, if the mortgage is for 30 years, you pay in 360 equal installments. (The last payment is often a few dollars more or less. This is opposed to a **Balloon Payment,** which is considerably larger than the rest.

Annual Percentage Rate (APR): The rate paid for a loan, including interest, loan fees, and points.

Appraisal: Evaluation of a property usually by a qualified appraiser, as required by most lenders. The amount of the appraisal is the maximum value on which the loan will be based. For example, if the appraisal is $100,000 and the lender loans 80 percent of value, the maximum mortgage will be $80,000.

ASA: American Society of Appraisers. A professional organization of appraisers.

As Is: A property sold without warrantees from the sellers. The sellers are essentially saying that they won't make any repairs.

Assignment of Mortgage: The lender's sale of a mortgage usually without the borrower's permission. For example, you may obtain a mortgage from XYZ Savings and Loan, which then sells the mortgage to Bland Bank. You will get a letter saying that the mortgage was assigned and you are to make your payments to a new entity. The document used between lenders for the transfer is the "assignment of mortgage."

Assumption: Taking over an existing mortgage. For example, a seller may have an assumable mortgage on a property. When you buy the property, you take over that seller's obligation under the loan. Today most fixed rate mortgages are not assumable. Most adjustable rate mortgages are, but the borrower must qualify. FHA and VA mortgages may be assumable if certain conditions are met. When you assume the mortgage, you may be personally liable if there is a foreclosure.

Automatic Guarantee: The power assigned to some lenders to guarantee VA loans without first checking with the Veterans Administration. These lenders can often make the loans quicker.

Backup: An offer that comes in after an earlier offer is accepted. If both buyer and seller agree, the backup assumes a secondary position, to be acted upon only if the original deal does not go through.

Balloon Payment: A single mortgage payment, usually the last, that is larger than all the others. In the case of second mortgages held by sellers, often only interest is paid until the due date—then the entire amount borrowed (the principal) is due. (See **Second Mortgage.**)

Biweekly Mortgage: A mortgage that is paid every other week instead of monthly. Since there are 52 weeks in the year, you end up making 26 payments, or the equivalent of one month's extra payment. The additional payments, applied to principal, significantly reduces the amount of interest charged on the mortgage and often reduces the term of the loan.

Blanket Mortgage: One mortgage that covers several properties instead of a single mortgage on each property. It is used most frequently by developers and builders.

Broker: An independent licensed agent, one who can establish his or her own office. Salespeople must work for brokers, typically for a few years, to get enough experience to become licensed as brokers.

Buyer's Agent: A real estate agent whose loyalty is to the buyer and not to the seller. Such agents are becoming increasingly common today.

Buy-Down Mortgage: A mortgage with a lower than market interest rate, either for the entire term of the mortgage or for a set period at the beginning—say, two years. The buy-down is made possible by the builder or seller paying an up-front fee to the lender.

Call Provision: A clause in a mortgage allowing the lender to call in the entire unpaid balance of the loan providing certain events have occurred, such as sale of the property. (See also **Acceleration Clause.**)

Canvas: To work a neighborhood, to go through it and knock on every door. Agents canvas to find listings. Investors and home buyers do it to find potential sellers who have not yet listed their property—and may agree to sell quickly for less.

Caps: Limits put on an adjustable rate mortgage. The interest rate, the monthly payment, or both may be capped.

Certificate of Reasonable Value (CRV): A document issued by the Veterans Administration establishing what the VA feels is the property's maximum value. In some cases, if you may pay more than this amount for the property, you will not qualify for the VA loan.

Chain of Title: The history of ownership of the property. The title to property forms a chain going back to the first owners, which in the Southwest, for example, may come from original Spanish land grants.

Closing: A transaction in which the seller conveys title to the buyer and the buyer makes full payment, including financing, for the property. At the closing, all required documents are signed and delivered and funds are disbursed.

Commission: The fee charged for an agent's services. Usually, but not always, the seller pays. There is no "set" fee; rather, the amount is fully negotiable.

Commitment: A written promise from lender to borrower offering a mortgage at a set amount, interest rate, and cost. Typically, commitments have a time limit—for example, they are good for 30 days or 45 days. Some lenders charge for making a commitment if you don't subsequently take out the mortgage (since they have tied up the money for that amount of time). When the lender's offer is in writing, it is sometimes called a "firm commitment."

Conforming Loan: A mortgage that conforms to the underwriting requirements of Fannie Mae and Freddie Mac.

Construction Loan: A mortgage made for the purpose of constructing a building. The loan is short-term, typically under 12 months, and is usually paid in installments directly to the builder as the work is completed. Most often, it is interest only.

Contingency: A condition that limits a contract. For example, the most common contingency says that a buyer is not required to complete a purchase if he or she fails to get necessary financing. (See also **Subject To.**)

Conventional Loan: Any loan that is not guaranteed or insured by the government.

Convertible Mortgage: An adjustable rate mortgage (ARM) with a clause allowing it to be converted to a fixed rate mortgage at some time in the future. You may have to pay an additional cost to obtain this type of mortgage.

Cosigner: Someone with better credit (usually a close relative) who agrees to sign your loan if you do not have good enough credit to qualify for a mortgage. The cosigner is equally responsible for repayment of the loan. (Even if you don't pay it back, the cosigner can be held liable for the entire balance.)

Credit Report: A report, usually from one of the country's three large credit reporting companies, that gives your credit history. It typically lists all your delinquent payments or failures to pay as well as any bankruptcies and, sometimes, foreclosures. Lenders use the report to determine whether to offer you a mortgage. The fee for obtaining the report is usually under $50, and you are charged for it.

Deal Point: Any point on which the deal hinges. It can be as important as the price or as trivial as changing the color of the mailbox.

Deposit: The money that buyers put up (also called "earnest money") to demonstrate their seriousness in making an offer. The deposit is usually at risk if the buyers fail to complete the transaction and have no acceptable way of backing out of the deal.

Disclosures: A list and explanation of features and defects in a property that sellers give to buyers. Most states now require disclosures.

Discount: The amount that a lender withholds from a mortgage to cover the points and fees. For example, you may borrow $100,000, but your points and fees come to $3,000; hence the lender will fund only $97,000, discounting the $3,000. Also, in the secondary market, a discount is the amount less than face value that a buyer of a mortgage pays in order to be induced to take out the loan. The discount here is calculated on the basis of risk, market rates, interest rate of the note, and other factors. (See **Points.**)

Dual Agent: An agent who expresses loyalty to both buyers and sellers and agrees to work with both. Only a few agents can successfully play this role.

Due-on-Encumbrance Clause: A little noted and seldom-enforced clause in recent mortgages that allows the lender to foreclose if the borrower gets additional financing. For example, if you secure a second mortgage, the lender of the first mortgage may have grounds for foreclosing. The reasoning here is that if you reduce your equity level by taking out additional financing, the lender may be placed in a less secure position.

Due-on-Sale Clause: A clause in a mortgage specifying that the entire unpaid balance becomes due and payable on sale of the property. (See **Acceleration Clause.**)

Escrow Company: An independent third party (stakeholder) that handles funds, carries out the instructions of the lender, buyer, and seller in a transaction, and deals with all the documents. In most states, companies are licensed to handle escrows. In some parts of the country, particularly the Northeast, the function of the escrow company may be handled by an attorney.

Fixed Rate Mortgage: A mortgage whose interest rate does not fluctuate for the life of the loan.

Fixer-Upper: A home that does not show well and is in bad shape. Often the property is euphemistically referred to in listings as a "TLC" (needs tender loving care) or "handyman's special."

FHA Loan: A mortgage insured by the Federal Housing Administration. In most cases, the FHA advances no money, but instead insures the loan to a lender such as a bank. There is a fee to the borrower, usually paid up front, for this insurance.

FSBO: For sale by owner.

Foreclosure: A legal proceeding in which the lender takes possession and title to a property, usually after the borrower fails to make timely payments on a mortgage.

Garbage Fees: Extra (and often unnecessary) charges tacked on when you obtain a mortgage.

Graduated-Payment Mortgage: A mortgage whose payments vary over the life of the loan. They start out low, then slowly rise until, usually after a few years, they reach a plateau where they remain for the balance of the term. Such a mortgage is particularly useful when you want low initial payments. It is primarily used by first-time buyers, often in combination with a fixed rate or adjustable rate mortgage.

Growing Equity Mortgage: A rarely used mortgage whose payments increase according to a set schedule. The purpose is to pay additional money into principal and thus pay off the loan earlier and save interest charges.

HOA: Home Owners Association, found mainly in condos but also in some single-family areas. It represents home owners and establishes and maintains neighborhood architectural and other standards. You usually must get permission from the HOA to make significant external changes to your property.

Index: A measurement of an established interest rate used to determine the periodic adjustments for adjustable rate mortgages. There are a wide variety of indexes, including the Treasury bill rates and the cost of funds to lenders.

Inspection: A physical survey of the property to determine if there are any problems or defects.

Jumbo: A mortgage for more than the maximum amount of a **Conforming Loan** (currently $240,000).

Lien: A claim for money against real estate. For example, if you had work done on your property and refused to pay the workperson, he or she might file a "mechanic's lien" against your property. If you didn't pay taxes, the taxing agency might file a "tax lien." These liens "cloud" the title and usually prevent you from selling the property or refinancing until they are cleared by paying off the debt.

Lock In: To tie up the interest rate for a mortgage in advance of actually getting it. For example, you might "lock in" your mortgage at 7.5 percent so that if rates subsequently rose, you would still get that rate.

Loan-to-Value Ratio (LTV): The percentage of the appraised value of a property that a lender will loan. For example, if your property appraises at $100,000 and the lender is willing to loan $80,000, the loan-to-value ratio is 80 percent.

Low-Ball: To make a very low initial offer to purchase.

MAI: Member, American Institute of Real Estate Appraisers. An appraiser with this designation has passed rigorous training.

Margin: An amount, calculated in points, that a lender adds to an index to determine how much interest you will pay during a period for an adjustable rate mortgage. For example, the index may be at 7 percent and the margin, agreed upon at the time you obtain the mortgage, may be 2.7 points. The interest rate for that period, therefore, is 9.7 percent. (See also **Index, Points.**)

Median Sales Price: The midpoint of the price of homes—as many properties are offered above this price as are offered below it.

MLS: Multiple Listing Service—used by **Realtors (R)** as a listings exchange. As much as 90 percent of all homes listed in the country are found on the MLS.

Mortgage: A loan arrangement between a borrower, or "mortgagor," and a lender, or "mortgagee." If you don't make your payments on a mortgage, the lender can foreclose, or take ownership of the property, only by going to court. This court action can take a great deal of time, often six months or more. Further, even after the lender has taken back the property, you may have an "equity of redemption" that allows you to redeem the property for years afterward, by paying back the mortgage and the lender's costs. The length of time it takes to foreclose, the costs involved, and the equity of redemption make a mortgage much less desirable to lenders than a **Trust Deed.**

Mortgage Banker: A lender that specializes in offering mortgages but none of the other services normally provided by a bank.

Mortgage Broker: A company that specializes in providing "retail" mortgages to consumers. It usually represents many different lenders.

Motivated Seller: A seller who has a strong desire to sell. For example, the seller may have been transferred and must move quickly.

Multiple Counteroffers: Comeback offers extended by the seller to several buyers simultaneously.

Multiple Offers: Offers submitted simultaneously from several buyers for the same property.

Negative Amortization: A condition arising when the payment on an adjustable rate mortgage is not sufficiently large to cover the interest charged. The excess interest is then added to the principal, so that the amount borrowed actually increases. The amount that the principal can increase is usually limited to 125 percent of the original mortgage value. Any mortgage that includes **Caps** has the potential to be negatively amortized.

Origination Fee: The total cost of obtaining a mortgage. Originally, it was a charge that lenders made for preparing and submitting a mortgage. The fee applied only to FHA and VA loans, which had to be submitted to the government for approval. With an FHA loan, the maximum origination fee was 1 percent.

Personal Property: Any property that does not go with the land. Such property includes automobiles, clothing, and most furniture. Some items such as appliances and floor and wall coverings are disputable. (See also **Real Property.**)

PITI: Principal, interest, taxes, and insurance. These are the major components that go into determining the monthly payment on a mortgage. (Other items include home owner's dues and utilities.)

Points: A point is 1 percent of a mortgage amount, payable on obtaining the loan. For example, if your mortgage is $100,000 and you are required to pay $2\frac{1}{2}$ points to get it, the charge to you is $2,500. Some points may be tax-deductible. Check with your accountant. A "basis point" is 1/100 of a point. For example. if you are charged $1/2$ point (0.5 percent of the mortgage), the lender will refer to it as 50 basis points.

Preapproval: Formal approval for a mortgage from a lender. You have to submit a standard application and have a credit check run. Also, the lender may require proof of income, employment, and money on deposit (to be used for the down payment and closing costs).

Prepayment Penalty: A charge made by the lender to the borrower for paying off a mortgage early. In times past (more than 25 years ago) nearly all mortgages carried prepayment penalties. However, those mortgages were also assumable by others. Today virtually no fixed rate mortgages (other than FHA or VA mortgages) are truly assumable and, hence, few carry a prepayment penalty clause. (See **Assumption.**)

Private Mortgage Insurance (PMI): Insurance that protects the lender in the event that the borrower defaults on a mortgage. It is written by an independent third-party insurance company and typically covers only the first 20 percent of the lender's potential loss. PMI is normally required on any mortgage that exceeds 80 percent **loan-to-value ratio.**

Purchase Money Mortgage: A mortgage obtained as part of the purchase price of a home (usually from the seller), as opposed to a mortgage obtained through refinancing. In some states, no deficiency judgment can be obtained against the borrower of a purchase money mortgage. (That is, if there is a foreclosure and the property brings less than the amount borrowed, the borrower cannot be held liable for the shortfall.)

Realtor (R): A broker who is a member of the National Association of Realtors. Agents who are not members may not use the Realtor designation.

Real Property: Real estate. This includes the land and anything appurtenant to it, including the house. Certain tests have been devised to determine whether an item is real property (goes with the land). For example, if curtains or drapes have been attached in such a way that they cannot be removed without damaging the home, they may be spoken of as real property. On the other hand, if they can easily be removed without damaging the home, they may be personal property. The purchase agreement should specify whether items are real or personal to avoid confusion later on.

RESPA: Real Estate Settlement Procedures Act. Legislation requiring lenders to provide borrowers with specified information on the cost of securing financing. Basically it means that before you proceed far along the path of getting the mortgage, the lender has to provide you with an estimate of costs. Then, before you sign the documents binding you to the mortgage, the lender has to provide you with a breakdown of the actual costs.

REO: Real estate owned—a term that refers to property taken back through foreclosure and held for sale by a lender.

Second Mortgage: An inferior mortgage usually placed on the property after a first mortgage. In the event of foreclosure, the second mortgage is paid off only after the first mortgage had been fully paid. Many lenders will not offer second mortgages.

Short sale: Property sale in which a lender agrees to accept less than the mortgage amount in order to facilitate the sale and avoid a foreclosure.

SREA: Society of Real Estate Appraisers—a professional association to which qualified appraisers can belong.

Subject To: A phrase often used to indicate that a buyer is not assuming the mortgage liability of a seller. For example, if the seller has an assumable loan and you (the buyer) "assume" the loan, you are taking over liability for payment. On the other hand, if you purchase "subject to" the mortgage, you do not assume liability for payment.

Subordination Clause: A clause in a mortgage document that keeps the mortgage subordinate to an existing mortgage. All the money from a foreclosure sale goes to pay off the lenders in order. Thus, the earlier the number of the mortgage (first, second, and so on), the more desirable and superior it is considered to be.

Title: Legal evidence that you actually have the right of ownership of **Real Property.** It is given in the form of a deed (there are many different types of deeds) that specifies the kind of title you have (joint, common, or other).

Title Insurance Policy: An insurance policy that covers the title to a home. It may list the owner or the lender as beneficiary. The policy is issued by a title insurance company and specifies that if for any covered reason your title proves defective, the company will correct the title or compensate you up to a specified amount, usually the amount of the purchase price or the mortgage.

Trust Deed: A three-party lending arrangement that includes a borrower, or "trustor"; an independent third-party stakeholder, or "trustee" (usually a title insurance company); and a lender, or "beneficiary" so-called because the lender stands to benefit if the trustee turns the deed over in case the borrower fails to make payments.

The advantage of the trust deed over the mortgage is that foreclosure can be accomplished without court action or deficiency judgment against the borrower. In other words, if the property is worth less than the loan, the lender can't come back to the borrower after the sale for the difference. (See also **Purchase Money Mortgage.**)

Upgrade: Any extra that a buyer may obtain when purchasing a new home—for example, a better-quality carpet or a wall mirror in the bedroom.

Upside Down: Owing more on a property than its market value.

VA Loan: A mortgage guaranteed by the Veterans Administration. The VA actually guarantees only a small percentage of the amount loaned, but since it guarantees the first monies loaned, lenders are willing to accept the arrangement. In a VA loan the government advances no money; rather, the mortgage is made by a private lender such as a bank.

Wraparound Financing: A blend of two mortgages, often used by sellers to get a higher interest rate or facilitate a sale. For example, instead of giving a buyer a simple **Second Mortgage,** the seller may combine the balance due on an existing mortgage (usually an existing first) with an additional loan. Thus the wrap includes both the second and the first mortgages. The borrower makes payments to the seller, who then keeps part of the payment and in turn pays off the existing mortgage.

Index

Accessibility, 11–12
Amenities, rental ratios and, 13–14
Amortization, 148
Application fees, 182
Appraisals, 69–70, 186, 194, 195
Architectural committee, 21
ARMs (adjustable-rate mortgages), 129–132, 144, 149, 195
"As is" homes, 50–53, 54, 79
ASHI (American Society of Home Inspectors), 90
Asking price, offering more than, 40–42
Assessments, home owners association, 21–22
Assessor's office, 113
Asset-based loans, 165–167
Assumption fees, 182
Attorney's fees, 176, 184
Auctions, 118–120
Automatic refinancing, 132

Backup position, in hot markets, 64–67
Balloon mortgages, 132, 148–149
Bankruptcy, 161
Banks, 3–4, 17, 28, 137, 166–167
    (*See also* Mortgages)
Bargains:
    in "as is" homes, 52
    at auctions, 118–120
    in creative financing, 161–164
    in fixer-uppers, 54–55, 56
    in foreclosures, 108, 113–117
    in FSBOS (for sale by owner) properties, 62–63
    in interest rates, 161
    in "out of favor" homes, 58–59
    in stock homes, 198–199
    with upside-down sellers, 121–124

Bidding wars:
    at auctions, 118
    avoiding, 43–45
    bugging out by sellers, 37–39
    offering more than asking price, 40–42
Biweekly mortgages, 132–133
Blanket mortgages, 169–170
Bugging out, by sellers, 37–39, 195, 196
Builders (*see* New homes)
Buy-downs, 160
Buyer's agents, 15–20
    bugging out by sellers and, 38–39
    cobroking deals, 16, 17, 18, 35
    commissions and, 15–19, 43, 182
    option to decide price paid, 43
Buying sight unseen, 47–49

California, 48, 90
Canvassing properties, 32–33
Caps, on ARMs, 130–131
Carry-back mortgages, 116
Cash deals, 2, 38–39, 68–71
CC&Rs (conditions, covenants, and restrictions), 21
Closing:
    long, 70
    negotiation after, 95–96
    short, 68
Closing costs, 176–187
    financing, 179–181
    garbage fees, 155–157, 182–187, 195
Closing review fees, 182
CLTV (combined loan to value), 181
Co-ops, 6, 13, 21, 22, 27
Cobroking deals, 16, 17, 18, 35
Cold markets, 28
    creative financing in, 164
    low-balling offers in, 110, 111–112

Cold markets, (*Cont.*):
  price/terms trade-off in, 101
  seller payment of closing costs,
    176–178
  stock homes in, 198–199
  stretching in, 106
Collateral, for asset-based loans,
  165–167
Commissions:
  buyer's agent and, 15–19, 43, 182
  as closing costs, 182
  saving, 32, 33
  seller's agent and, 15–19
  split, 16, 17, 18, 35
  upside-down sellers and, 123
Comprehensive sales agreements, 115
Condominiums, 6, 13–14, 27
Conforming loans, 127, 133–134, 185
Consolidating debt, 169–170
Contingencies, 77–82
  in buying sight unseen, 48–49
  clear title and title insurance, 119
  deadline for purchase completion,
    79, 81
  deal points in, 79–80
  disclosures (*see* Disclosures)
  inspections (*see* Inspections)
Convertible mortgages, 149
Cosmetic improvements, 56, 58–59
Cost-free mortgages, 144
Counteroffers, 41, 44–45, 92, 93
Courier fees, 183
Creative financing techniques,
  26, 161–164
Credit reports, 2, 3, 69, 124, 126, 134,
  151–152, 161, 183
Credit unions, 3–4
Crime, 5, 9–10, 27, 33

Damages, 70–71
Deal points, 79–80
Debt forgiven, 124
Deed, 21, 114, 117
Defective properties:
  "as is" homes, 50–53, 79
  buying sight unseen, 48
  fixer-uppers, 54–56

Defective properties, (*Cont.*):
  low-ball offers for, 111
  negotiation after closing, 95–96
  (*See also* Inspections)
Deposits:
  in cash deals, 68, 70–71
  down payments and, 85–86, 87
  early offers and, 46
  in escrow, 84, 85–86
  increasing size of, 87
  on new homes, 192, 194–195, 199
  refund of, 78
  risk of losing, 83–84
  small, 83–87
  withdrawal of, 84
Design centers, 201, 202
Developers (*see* New homes)
Disclosures, 78, 87
  for "as is" homes, 51, 52
  at auctions, 119
  in buying sight unseen, 48–49
  for FSBOs, 60, 63
  need for, 89
  negotiating, 92–93
  obtaining, 90
Discount points, 183
Document drawing/signing fees, 183
Document preparation fees, 183
Double-escrowing, 196
Down payments:
  absence of, 161
  at auctions, 119
  deposits and, 85–86, 87
  early offers and, 46
  minimizing, 108
  size of mortgage and, 103
  standard size, 180
"Dual" agents, 16

Early offers, 32–33, 46
Earnest money (*see* Deposits)
Education (*see* Schools)
Electronic mortgages, 3–4, 103,
  133–134, 140
Escrow, 84, 85–86, 94–95, 155, 176, 196
Escrow charges, 183–184, 186
Exclusivity, 19, 34, 35–36

Fannie Mae (FNMA), 116, 127, 134, 136, 185
"Farming" properties, 32–33
Federal Housing Administration (FHA), 116, 128, 134–135, 163, 184–185
Federal Trade Commission (FTC), 143
Fee-for-service brokers, 33, 62
FICO (Fair Isaac), 126
Financing closing costs, 179–181
Fire insurance, 184
Fixed-rate mortgages, 128–129
Fixer-uppers, 54–56
"For sale by owner" (FSBO) properties, 17, 35, 60–63
Foreclosures, 108, 113–117, 161, 173
125 per cent loans and, 152–153
REO market, 115–117
short sales and, 122
Freddie Mac, 69, 116, 127, 134, 136, 185
FSBOs (for sale by owner), 17, 35, 60–63, 123

Garbage fees, 155–157, 182–187, 195
Gated communities, 9
Government insured or guaranteed loans, 116, 126, 127, 128, 134–135, 136, 163, 184–185
Graffiti Index, 10

Handyman's special, 54–56
Home description sheets, 23–24
Home equity mortgages, 56, 135, 145, 153
Home owners association (HOA), 21–22, 59
Hot markets, 27–28, 32–71
"as is" homes, 50–53
avoiding bidding wars, 43–45
backup position, 64–67
buying sight unseen, 47–49
canvassing properties in, 32–33
cash offers, 68–71
early offers, 32–33, 46
elusive sellers in, 37–39
finding agents for, 34–36

Hot markets (*Cont.*):
fixer-uppers, 54–56
"for sale by owner" homes, 60–63
new homes in, 190–197
offering more than asking price, 40–42
"out of favor" homes, 57–59
price/terms trade-off in, 101
stock homes in, 198
stretching in, 106, 107

Impounds, 184
Index, on ARMs, 130, 131–132
Inspections, 60, 63, 78, 81
of "as is" homes, 51–53
of auctioned properties, 119
buying sight unseen, 48–49
cash settlements following, 94
need for, 88–89
negotiating, 93–94
obtaining, 89–90
(*See also* Defective properties)
Insurance:
fire, 184
mortgage, 184–185
(*See also* Title insurance)
Interest rates:
on ARMs, 129–132
on asset-based loans, 166
below-market, 161
on blanket mortgages, 169–170
on fixed-rate mortgages, 128–129
on jumbo mortgages, 136
lock-ins, 141–143
on low-doc, no-doc loans and, 173–174
on 125 per cent loans, 154
for prime borrowers, 126–127
for subprime borrowers, 127–128
term of mortgage and, 147–150
trading points for, 158–160
Internet lenders, 3–4, 103, 133–134, 140

Judicial mortgages, 117
Jumbo mortgages, 136

Landscaping, 58–59
Lawyers, real estate, 33, 62, 78–79
Lenders:
  and financing of closing costs,
    179–181
  government insured or guaranteed,
    116, 126–128, 134–136, 163,
    184–185
  "legitimate," 3–4
  new home financing by, 195
  preapprovals with (*see* Preapproval
    letters)
  rental ratios and, 13
  REO market, 115–117
  RESPA and, 139–140, 157, 182
  short sales and, 122–124
  (*See also* Mortgages)
Lender's attorney's fees, 184
Lender's escrow, 184
Liens, 114, 115
Lifestyle, location and, 5–6
Lines of credit, 135
Loan origination fee, 139–140
Loan-to-value (LTV) ratio, 151, 162,
  179–181, 184
Location, 5–6
  crime and, 5, 9–10, 27, 33
  new homes and, 190
  in plan of action, 27
  rental ratio and, 5, 13–14
  schools and, 5, 7–8, 27
  shopping and, 5, 11–12, 27, 58
  transportation and, 5, 11–12, 27
Lock-ins, 141–143
Low-balling offers, 110–112
Low-doc mortgages, 172–174
LTV (loan to value), 151, 162,
  179–181, 184

Maps, 23–25
Margin, on ARMs, 130
Market knowledge, 27–28
  cold markets, 28
  hot markets, 27–28, 32–71
  normal markets, 28
  real estate maps and, 24–25
Marketable title, 63

Median home price, 8
Mortgage(s), 126–136
  ARMs, 129–132, 144, 149, 195
  asset-based, 165–167
  assuming existing, 128, 182
  balloon, 132, 148–149
  biweekly, 132–133
  blanket, 169–170
  carry-back, 116
  convertible, 149
  cost-free, 144
  electronic, 3–4, 103, 133–134, 140
  fixed rate, 128–129
  garbage fees, 155–157, 182–187, 195
  government-insured or guaranteed,
    116, 126–128, 134–136, 163,
    184–185
  home equity, 56, 135, 145, 153
  jumbo, 136
  lock-ins, 141–143
  low-doc, no-doc, 172–174
  negative amortization, 131
  125 per cent, 131, 151–154
  in other properties, 168–170
  preapprovals (*see* Preapproval
    letters)
  prepayment penalties, 144–146
  prime borrowers, 126–127
  RESPA and, 139–140, 157, 182
  second, 101, 102, 135, 153, 163,
    168–170, 180
  subprime borrowers, 127–128
  term of, 147–150
  of upside-down sellers, 121–124,
    152–153
  yield on, 155–156
Mortgage bankers, 3–4, 137, 166
Mortgage brokers, 3–4, 126, 134,
  137–140, 142, 161, 166, 170
Mortgage insurance, 184–185
Motivated sellers:
  analysis of, 97–100
  defective properties and, 111
  price/terms trade-off and, 101–104
  seller financing by, 119, 128, 161–164
  upside-down, 121–124, 152–153
Multiple counteroffers, 44–45

Multiple listing services, 34, 35, 115
Multiple-offer sales (*see* Bidding wars)

NAHI (National Association of
    Home Inspectors), 90
Negative amortization, 131
Negotiation, 92–96
    of contingencies, 79–80
    of disclosures, 92–93
    of garbage fees, 186–187
    for new homes, 196
    seller payment of closing
        costs, 176–178
    of upgrades, 201–202
Neighborhood (*see* Location)
Neighborhood beautification
    programs, 59
Neighbors, and motivation of
    sellers, 99
New homes, 190–202
    being first in line for, 190–197
    buy-downs, 160
    model units, 191, 192
    stock homes, 198–199
    upgrades, 195–196, 201–202
No-doc mortgages, 172–174
Normal markets:
    characteristics of, 28, 40–41
    creative financing in, 164
    low-balling offers in, 110
    multiple offers in, 43
    seller payment of closing costs,
        176–178
    stock homes in, 198–199
    stretching in, 107

Offers, 74–104
    on "as-is" homes, 53
    counteroffers, 41, 44–45, 92, 93
    deadlines for acceptance, 74–76
    low-balling first, 110–112
    more than asking price, 40–42
    negotiating, 92
    price/terms trade-off in, 101–104
    rejection of, 75
On-line lenders, 3–4, 103, 133–134, 140
125 per cent loans, 131, 151–154

Origination fees, 185
"Out of favor" homes, 57–59
Overextension, 108–109

Payment cap, 131
Piggyback mortgages, 136
Plan of action, 26–30
Points, 139–140, 155–156, 176, 195
    in buy-downs, 160
    in creative financing, 162
    discount, 183
    trading for interest, 158–160
Police department, 9–10
Portfolio loans, 136
Preapproval letters, 2–4
    bugging out by sellers and, 38–39
    in cash deals, 69
    early offers and, 32–33, 46
    importance of, 2, 26
    new homes and, 192, 196
    small deposits and, 86–87
    in stretching for more expensive
        property, 106
Prepayment penalties, 144–146
Price:
    in bidding wars, 37–45, 118
    of fixer-uppers, 54–55
    geographic location and, 107
    in housing slumps, 112
    median home, 8
    of new homes, 193–194
    in plan of action, 26
    price/terms trade-off, 101–104
    stretching for more expensive
        property, 106–108
    upside-down sellers and, 121–124,
        152–153
    (*See also* Bargains; Cold markets; Hot
        markets; Normal markets)
Prime borrowers, 126–127
Principals, 32–33
Purchase agreements, 60
    in buying sight unseen, 48–49
    in canvassing properties, 33
    in cash deals, 68–69
    early offers and, 32–33, 46
    (*See also* Contingencies)

Quit claim deeds, 114

Real estate board, 28
Real estate brokers:
 buyer's agents (*see* Buyer's agents)
 cobroking deals, 16, 17, 18, 35
 exclusive use of, 19, 34, 35–36
 fee-for-service, 33, 62
 FSBOs (for sale by owner), 60
 functions of, 60
 home description sheets, 23–24
 listing agents, 18, 34–36, 39
 locating trustworthy, 34–36
 for REOs, 115–117
 seller's agents (*see* Seller's agents)
 (*See also* Commissions)
Real estate maps, 23–25
Recording fees, 176
Recreational property, 14, 27
Recurring costs, 176
Rent-backs, 102
Rental property, 168–170
Rental ratio, 5, 13–14
REOs, 115–117
Repossessions, 17, 28
Resale:
 accessibility and, 11
 buy-downs in, 160
 home owners association and, 22
 neighborhood beautification
  programs, 59
 of new homes, 196–197
 rental ratios and, 13–14
Reserves, at auctions, 118–119
RESPA (Real Estate Settlement
 Procedures Act), 139–140,
  157, 182

Sales agreements, 115
Savings and loan associations (S&Ls),
  3–4, 137
Schools, 5, 7–8, 27
Second homes, 14, 27
Second mortgages, 101, 102, 135,
  153, 163, 168–170, 180

Self-employment, 171–174
Sellers:
 bugging out by, 37–39, 195, 196
 financing by, 119, 128, 161–164
 motivation of (*see* Motivated sellers)
 payment of closing costs, 176–178
 price/terms trade-off and, 101–104
 rent-backs to, 102
 upside-down, 121–124, 152–153
Seller's agents, 15–19
 bugging out by sellers and, 38–39,
  195, 196
 cobroking deals, 16, 17, 18, 35
 commissions and, 15–19
 deadlines for offers, 76
 "dual" agents, 16
 exclusivity and, 19, 34, 35–36
 home description sheets, 23–24
 motivation of sellers, 98
 offering more than asking price,
  40–42
 substantial defects contingency, 49
Shopping, 5, 11–12, 27, 58
Short sales, 122–124
Single-family homes, 27
Specific performance, 70, 78
Stock homes, 198–199
Stretching for home purchase,
  106–108
Subject-to's (*see* Contingencies)
Subletting, 13–14
Subprime borrowers, 127–128
Substantial defects, 49

Taxes:
 confirmation of income with IRS,
  171, 172, 173
 on debt forgiven, 124
 on home equity mortgages, 135
 and seller payment of closing
  costs, 178
 on upside-down sellers, 153–154
Teasers, 129
Tenants, 13–14
Term of mortgage, 147–150

Time limits:
  for accepting offers, 74–76
  on backup positions, 65
  on contingencies, 79, 81
  for home listings, 19
  on multiple counteroffers, 44–45
Title insurance, 113, 116–117, 119,
  123–124, 155, 176, 183, 184, 186
Townhouses, 6, 27
Transportation, 5, 11–12, 27
Trust deeds, 117

Underwriting review fees, 185
Up-front fees, 17–19

Upgrades, 195–196, 201–202
Upside-down sellers, 121–124,
  152–153

Vacation homes, 14, 27
Vest pocket listings, 35
Veterans' Administration
  (VA), 116, 128,
  134–135, 163

Walk-throughs, 78, 91
Warehousing fees, 185

Yield, 155–156, 159–160

About the Author

Robert Irwin, one of America's leading experts in all areas of real estate, is the author of more than twenty books, including McGraw-Hill's best-selling *Tips and Traps* series. He lives in Rancho Palos Verdes, California.